Skinny Meals in Heels

Jennifer Joyce

Skinny Meals in Heels

Prep-Ahead, Figure-Friendly Dishes
for the Busy Home Chef

ATRIA PAPERBACK

New York   London   Toronto   Sydney   New Delhi

Contents

Diet is a dirty word

Make no mistake, this is NOT a diet book. Nor is it a mundane "health" cookbook stripped of fat and all the fun. Envisage instead a collection of quick mouthwatering recipes that "happen" to be low in fat; vinaigrettes, chilis and spices supersede butter sauces, and baking replaces frying. Eating bacon, cheese and nuts is still encouraged, albeit in smaller, lean amounts. Trust me, this is "healthy meets delicious cooking" and you won't feel deprived or hungry.

Though not intentional, my lean piquant food is truly the way I like to eat. My Italian mother initiated me with the wonders of olive oil and since then my love for food has continued to evolve from my lifelong obsession with travel. It didn't take me long to discover the magic of Asian sauces, spice pastes and fresh aromatic herbs. These star ingredients galvanize your taste buds with their salty, sour and pungent tastes. Practically anything can be made wondrous with them and, best of all, they aren't fattening.

Time is of the essence in everyone's world, so most of these 130+ recipes can be made in 30 minutes or under 1 hour. Quick, delicious and healthy is the new cooking mantra for today's busy lives.

So cook your friends or family a guilt-free glamorous meal, and don't forget a glass of wine. It doesn't matter if you're wearing heels or slippers.

Jennifer Joyce

Skinny Tips

DON'T DIET, DON'T DENY YOURSELF...
JUST THINK SKINNY

It's been proven that exercise alone won't make you lose weight
— it's all about what you eat. You don't have to count the calories
or the fat, just use your common sense and judiciously cut back
the fat. I still enjoy fried food, a creamy dessert or roast on
the weekend, but not every day. Making skinny, delicious food
midweek will vastly improve your diet and it doesn't mean
missing out on flavor or a satisfying quantity. Here are some
practical guidelines to smarter eating.

DON'T EAT BETWEEN MEALS
Snacking is one of the biggest reasons for weight gain. It keeps
you from gauging whether you're hungry, full or just bored. If
you change one thing ... THIS IS IT! Eat three meals that include
protein of some sort and you won't need to snack. It also gives
your body a chance to burn off the calories you've eaten already.
When the next meal rolls around, you'll most certainly be hungry.
Food always tastes better when you're starving. Making sure
you have protein in every meal is vital to making this work,
otherwise you may feel tortured.

QUIT WHEN YOU'RE FULL
There isn't a law that says you have to finish your plate. Forget
what your mother said when your stomach says "full." STOP!
Overeating stretches your stomach and will increase your
appetite. It's important to know when you're hungry or full,

and overeating confuses your stomach and brain. Later on, lethargy and nausea come into play, but then it's too late. Likewise, if you don't feel hungry at breakfast, don't feel that you have to eat. Wait until later in the morning and then eat. Your body will tell you when it's ready.

DON'T DENY YOURSELF THE GOOD TASTES

We all love the taste of bacon, feta cheese or a dollop of cream in food, and there is no reason why you should stop — just use far less. Instead of eight slices of bacon in a stew, use two. You will get all the smoky taste but not as much saturated fat. Same goes for cheese; instead of using half a block of Parmesan or feta, just use a couple of tablespoons sprinkled over. It's vital in recipes to include a bit of these flavors, otherwise healthy cooking becomes a bit earnest and dull.

WINE AND COFFEE

You will be glad to know these favorites can help you — within reason of course. Both suppress your appetite, so if you're making dinner and want to devour a large slice of bread with butter, have a glass of wine instead. (Just don't drink the whole bottle before you tuck in.) Likewise, if you can't wait for lunch, drink a cup of coffee or tea. It will stave off hunger pains.

GOOD FAT VERSUS BAD FAT

There are two types of fat, saturated and unsaturated. Animal fat is the former and that's the area you want to considerably cut back on. Butter, cream, bacon and sausages are all in that list so keep them to a minimum if you can. Monounsaturated and polyunsaturated fats are the virtuous types, and these include:

olive oil, vegetable oils, nuts, olives and avocado. Although
still high in calories, they won't give you cholesterol. Your
body still needs fat to maintain a nutritional balance, so keep
cooking with these.

VEGETABLES AND FRUIT
Nutritionists say you should eat five servings of fruit or veg a day
and the brighter the color the better. It's not always possible, and
I certainly don't keep count. But consider throwing some spinach,
green beans or other quick-cooking vegetable into your main dish
if it works. It saves washing another pot and you get a bit more
health into your diet. Eating raw vegetables is also important, so
toss a little side salad together or eat a raw carrot while cooking.
The extra fiber keeps your gut clean and helps wipe out toxins
left in the body.

VARY WHAT YOU EAT
Eat a wide variety of foods so that you can take in all the
nutrients your body needs. Make a grains salad every couple
of weeks, boil lentils instead of rice, go vegetarian a few nights
or try tofu. Avoid cooking the same things over and over, such as
pasta or steak. It's good to have red meat one night, but not three
times a week. Avoid too many sandwiches for lunch, and vary
it with main-dish salads or hearty soups. Cooking seasonally also
encourages you to cook a variety of vegetables, fish and fruit. It
costs much less and is more environmentally friendly
than using nonseasonal foods.

FOLLOW THE EXAMPLE OF THE FRENCH AND ITALIANS

If you eat something rich at home or in a restaurant, then make sure you eat vegetables or salad with it. Although the Italians and French indulge in fried foods, rich meats and creamy cheese as part of their wonderful cuisines, they also consume a vast array of vegetables and fruit. Salad is eaten after nearly every meal. Overweight people are rarely seen in these countries because of their common-sense eating, legume-rich diet, minimal snacking and love of seasonal vegetables.

USE YOUR FREEZER MORE

We all have nights when we lose the will to cook. Sometimes it's too late, you're tired and takeout is just a phone call away. The next time you cook something healthy, make double and freeze the other portion. If you marinate meat or poultry for grilling, freeze a few extra pieces with the sauce. When it thaws, it will soak up all the lovely flavors and will be ready to barbecue. Freeze leftover rice in zip-lock bags and use it for fried rice.

STOCK UP YOUR KITCHEN WITH GOOD FOOD

If you want to eat well, a little shopping and planning is required. Stock up your pantry and freezer with core basics to cook with and your weekly shop won't be so arduous. Have a decent selection of spices, Asian ingredients, vinegars and oils so that you don't have to scramble midweek to find them. Make a big grocery trip once a week with a few dinners planned and buy some fresh vegetables to use ad hoc. For the nights you're not organized, use the pantry to pull from and whip up risottos, chicken dishes, stir-fries with noodles, or a big main-course salad.

KEY INGREDIENTS

FREEZE Chicken, meat, fish, peas, corn, lavash bread, edamame and fresh bread crumbs.

PANTRY Lentils, cans of chickpeas or beans, pasta, polenta, canned tomatoes, tuna, basmati rice, risotto rice, Asian dried noodles, potatoes, onions, garlic, shallots, dried fruits (including apricots, raisins and prunes), vegetable broth powder, honey, a wide variety of spices, salt, pepper, a variety of vinegars and oils, olives, capers, anchovies, white wine, Dijon mustard and grainy mustard, and flour.

REFRIGERATOR Greek-style yogurt, eggs, feta, Parmesan, nuts, tofu, limes, lemon, red and green chiles, fresh gingerroot, mangoes, tomato or lime chutney, sliced roast turkey or chicken and bags of lettuce.

SPICE PASTES AND ASIAN SAUCES

Harissa, chile bean paste, Thai red curry paste, Indian curry paste, miso, hoisin sauce, oyster sauce, soy sauce, mirin, rice vinegar and Thai sweet chile sauce.

Nearly all these pastes and sauces stay fresh for more than a year, so even though you may only use a tiny amount, they will keep for a long time. Once opened, they should be kept in the refrigerator, with the exception of soy and vinegar.

KITCHEN EQUIPMENT

There are certain items that can help you cook with less fat.
The most important is a good-quality nonstick skillet.
Buy a brand with a thick heavy bottom that distributes heat
evenly while cooking.

Next is a large heavy-bottomed saucepan. If you cook onions
slowly in them, then not as much oil is required.

Other useful items include: pastry brush for brushing oil,
spray oil mister, cast iron grill pan, glass jam jars for making
vinaigrettes, citrus zester, electric spice grinder, mortar and
pestle, large shallow baking dishes, large baking sheets,
fine-mesh sieve and, of course, a good sharp chopping knife.

Snacks & Nibbles

Oven-dried cherry tomatoes with lemon-oregano salt

preparation time 10 minutes / **cooking time** 1½ hours / **makes** 2 cups

Oven-drying has been an epiphany for me while writing this book. The flavors of oven-dried vegetables and fruit intensify for a powerful taste. Lemon-oregano salt makes these cherry tomatoes taste like heaven. Unlike most dehydrating, you don't need to dry these overnight, only 1½ hours on very low heat.

14 ounces baby plum tomatoes
finely grated zest of 1 lemon
2 teaspoons dried wild oregano
2 cloves garlic, thinly sliced
1 teaspoon sea salt

Preheat the oven to 200°F.
Halve the tomatoes and place, cut side up, on a baking sheet. Mix together the lemon zest, oregano, garlic and salt. Sprinkle over the tomatoes. Place in the oven for 1½ hours or until semi-dried. They are ready to eat or add to salads.

PREP AHEAD

These will keep for 1 week in the refrigerator in an airtight container.

THE SKINNY

There is absolutely no oil used, which means no fat. Tomatoes are packed with lycopene, an antioxidant that wards off disease.

Little pickled vegetables

preparation time 15 minutes / cooking time 5 minutes / pickling time 28 hours / makes 4 cups

There is nothing like a crunchy pickled vegetable with a hint of sweetness and the tang of vinegar. I have tried many variations of pickles and the key to a crisp texture is salting the vegetables beforehand. You don't need to properly bottle these because they won't last that long. Just pour them into a glass or plastic container and refrigerate for 24 hours.

3 zucchini, cut into ⅓-inch-thick slices
6 sweet baby bell peppers
   cut into fat rings
1 large cucumber, seeds removed and
   cut into chunks
1 yellow onion, thickly sliced
4 tablespoons sea salt

Pickling liquid
2 cups cider vinegar
1⅜ cups superfine sugar
2 tablespoons yellow mustard seeds
1 large pinch of chile flakes

Mix all the vegetables with the salt, place in a sieve over a bowl and leave for 4 hours or overnight in the refrigerator.

Rinse them well afterwards and place in a 4-cup capacity glass jar with a lid.

To make the pickling liquid, place all the ingredients in a saucepan over medium heat and bring to a boil. Cook for 5 minutes until slightly syrupy. Pour over the vegetables, cool, then cover and refrigerate. Leave to pickle for at least 24 hours.

PREP AHEAD

These will keep for 1 week in the refrigerator in an airtight container.

THE SKINNY

Pickles of any sort make a healthy low-calorie snack. If using store-bought versions, then be sure they aren't too high in sodium.

Spicy pumpkin and sunflower seeds

preparation time 5 minutes / **cooking time** 15 minutes / **makes** 1¼ cups

If you want a quick nibble that's healthy and tasty, these spicy salted seeds will satisfy your peckish cravings. Use to sprinkle on salads as well.

1 cup pumpkin seeds
3 tablespoons sunflower seeds
1 tablespoon olive oil
1 teaspoon smoked paprika
1 teaspoon superfine sugar
1 teaspoon sea salt

Preheat the oven to 350°F. Mix all the ingredients together in a bowl and spread in a single layer on a baking sheet. Bake for 10–15 minutes or until golden at the edges. Remove and cool.

PREP AHEAD

These will keep for 2 weeks in an airtight container.

THE SKINNY

Healthful and high in fiber, these make a spicy nibble to have with a drink — much better than chips.

Oven-dried root vegetable chips

preparation time 15 minutes / **cooking time** 1¼ hours / **makes** 2 cups

I know it sounds ridiculous to make your own chips, but these will have you hooked. Forget that these are skinny snacks — the concentrated taste of the vegetables with a sprinkle of sea salt is glorious. I tried many cooking methods when making these and low heat works best. If baked at higher temperatures, they don't cook evenly and burn at the edges. Making your own is easy, but it's advisable to pick up a mandoline to slice them; the cheap plastic versions work fine and stay sharp for a long time.

2 beets, scrubbed and unpeeled
2 parsnips, scrubbed and unpeeled
1 sweet potato, scrubbed
    and unpeeled
1½ tablespoons vegetable oil, for oiling
sea salt

Preheat the oven to 225°F. Using a mandoline, slice the vegetables to about ⅛ inch thick. Place on oiled baking sheets in a single layer and sprinkle with sea salt. Cook for 1¼ hours or until the slices start to curl up around the edges. As all ovens differ slightly, keep an eye on the chips during the last 10 minutes of cooking. Even if they are slightly chewy in the center, when you remove them, they will crisp up on cooling. Remove from the oven, cool, then store immediately in an airtight container.

PREP AHEAD

Store in an airtight container for 2–3 days.

THE SKINNY

Oven-drying is a useful way to crisp up fruits and vegetables. Store-bought versions can be very expensive and potentially full of fat and sugar. These are an ideal skinny snack to replace chips and other junk food.

Turkish pepper and feta salsa with pita chips

preparation time 20 minutes / cooking time 10 minutes / makes 2 cups

This finely diced Middle Eastern salsa incorporates all the sweet, sour and salty tastes we crave. Scoop up bites with crisp baked pita triangles for a guilt-free treat. The key is to cut everything up nice and tiny so it picks up the other flavors.

Pita chips

6 pita breads
olive oil spray
1 tablespoon sumac or mild ground chile
   pepper (optional)
sea salt
black pepper

Turkish pepper and feta salsa

2 tablespoons pomegranate molasses
1 tablespoon tomato paste
1 small bell red pepper, finely diced
1 small cucumber, seeds removed
   and finely diced
1 small red onion, finely diced
2 tablespoons finely chopped mint
2 tablespoons crumbled feta cheese

To make the pita chips, preheat the oven to 400°F. Using a pair of scissors, cut around the edges of the pita bread and remove. Cut the remaining part into large rectangles and pull apart. Place on a baking sheet and spray with the olive oil. Sprinkle with sea salt, freshly ground black pepper and sumac or chili powder. Bake for 8–10 minutes or until golden. Remove and cool.

Meanwhile, make the salsa. Mix the pomegranate molasses and tomato paste in a bowl and season. Mix in the remaining ingredients. Serve with the pita chips.

PREP AHEAD

The pita chips can be stored for 3 days in an airtight container. The salsa can be covered and refrigerated for 1 day.

THE SKINNY

Baked pita chips have little oil and far fewer calories than potato chips or tortilla chips, making them a much healthier option. Olive oil sprays are a great buy because it means you don't need to use much oil when cooking.

Padrón peppers with honey and paprika

preparation time 5 minutes / cooking time 5 minutes / serves 4

Padrón peppers are tiny and green with a mild taste, but be warned, there is always one spicy one per bag. Flash-fry them in a hot skillet and serve straight up. Hold them by their stem to bite off the warm pepper.

1 tablespoon olive oil
7 ounces Padrón peppers
1 tablespoon honey
1 teaspoon sherry vinegar
½ teaspoon smoked paprika
sea salt

Heat the oil in a skillet until nearly smoking hot. Add the peppers and allow to sizzle for 3 or so minutes. They will puff up and brown, so toss them around in the skillet a bit so they don't burn. Transfer to a platter.

Mix the honey and vinegar together and drizzle over the peppers. Sprinkle with the paprika and season with sea salt.

PREP AHEAD

The peppers should be cooked just before serving.

THE SKINNY

Padrón and other pan-fried peppers are healthful and make a quick skinny bite.

Tarragon-marinated baby mushrooms

preparation time 5 minutes / marinating time 30 minutes / makes 2 cups

These button mushrooms are infused with a zingy lemon, tarragon and sherry vinegar dressing. Serve with other antipasti or on their own with bread.

7 ounces small button mushrooms, trimmed
1 clove garlic
juice of ½ lemon
1 tablespoon chopped tarragon
1 tablespoon Champagne vinegar or good-quality white wine vinegar
1 tablespoon extra virgin olive oil

Toss all the ingredients together in a bowl. Leave to marinate at room temperature for 30 minutes.

Just before serving, toss a couple of times to coat everything. Remove the clove garlic. Serve the mushrooms with little toothpicks.

PREP AHEAD

The mushrooms can be made 1 day ahead, covered and refrigerated.

THE SKINNY

Marinated mushrooms are healthy nibbles that are skimpy on calories.

Marinated olives with fennel, lemon and celery

preparation time 10 minutes / **makes** 1½ cups

My mother used to buy a mix of this sort from our Italian deli and I loved picking out the tangy onions and celery. Oil-cured olives are preferable over Kalamata or other brined varieties as they have less salt and a milder flavor.

1 cup oil-cured black olives
2 celery ribs, from the heart,
   thinly sliced
½ small red onion, chopped
1 tablespoon finely grated lemon zest
1 tablespoon extra virgin olive oil
1 tablespoon red wine vinegar
1 teaspoon fennel seeds

Mix all the ingredients together in a small bowl and serve.

PREP AHEAD

These will keep for 1 week in the refrigerator in an airtight container.

THE SKINNY

Yes, olives are high in fat, but "fat" doesn't always mean fattening. Olives have the good kind of fat, monounsaturated, which is beneficial for your heart. You're not going to eat this whole portion yourself — it's meant to be a little bite to have with drinks.

Spiced garlic flat bread

preparation time 5 minutes / cooking time 10 minutes / makes 16

If you're serving up a Middle Eastern meal, this fragrant bread can be made in less than 10 minutes.

1 tablespoon olive oil
2 large pieces lavash bread
1 clove garlic, finely chopped
1 tablespoon za'atar or
   Middle Eastern spice mix
2 tablespoons finely chopped flat-leaf
   (Italian) parsley
sea salt
black Pepper

Preheat the oven to 400°F. Brush the olive oil over the flat breads and scatter with the garlic, spices and some sea salt and freshly ground black pepper. Place on a baking sheet and cook for 7–8 minutes or until crisp at the edges. Scatter the parsley over them and cut into triangles.

PREP AHEAD

The flat bread can be prepared, unbaked, on the morning of serving and heated just before you're ready to eat.

THE SKINNY

Spice mixes are indispensable for making quick mezze. Along with the garlic, the spice mix used here elevates the flat bread into a warm intoxicating snack.

Shrimp cocktail

preparation time 5 minutes / serves 4

With a dipping sauce spiked with horseradish and ketchup, there's no denying the retro allure of a shrimp cocktail! Say hello to this skinny classic.

10 tablespoons ketchup
1 tablespoon shredded fresh horseradish
   or store-bought horseradish cream
1 lemon, juiced to yield 1 teaspoon
   and the rest quartered into wedges
1 tablespoon finely chopped celery
1 teaspoon Worcestershire sauce
½ teaspoon hot pepper sauce
1–2 heads Boston lettuce,
   leaves separated
¾ pound cooked peeled
   large shrimp
sea salt
black pepper

Mix together the ketchup, horseradish, lemon juice, celery and Worcestershire and hot pepper sauces in a small bowl and season with sea salt and freshly ground black pepper.

Arrange the lettuce and lemon wedges on a platter or plate and top with the shrimp. Serve the cocktail sauce alongside.

PREP AHEAD

All the components can be prepared 1 day ahead, refrigerated, then assembled the following day.

THE SKINNY

Shrimp are full of protein to fill you up and have almost no fat.

Crisp tofu bites with chile soy-vinegar sauce

preparation time 10 minutes / cooking time 5 minutes / makes 32

Before I wrote this book I have to admit that I never loved tofu. Deep-fried, perhaps, but in no other manner. This Chinese preparation changed my mind and now I'm a convert. There are two types of tofu: silken and firm. The former is delicate and wobbly like jelly and is mostly steamed or used in soups. Firm is usually seared or fried because, once drained, it can withstand heat without falling apart. The key is to drain it extremely well before cooking so you get a crisp edge.

1 package firm tofu (12 ounces)
1 tablespoon sesame seeds
1 tablespoon sesame oil
1 red bird's eye chile, seeds removed
    and finely chopped
1 tablespoon soy sauce
1 tablespoon Chinese black
    or red wine vinegar
1 teaspoon superfine sugar
2 scallions, finely chopped

Wrap the tofu with lots of paper towels. Press firmly to remove all the excess water. You may need to do this a couple of times to get all the water out. Halve the tofu horizontally, then cut each piece into 16 cubes. Toss with the sesame seeds.

Heat the sesame oil in a nonstick skillet until very hot. Add the tofu and brown at least 2–3 minutes, about 1 minute each side. Use 2 teaspoons or a pair of chopsticks to turn them over when browned. Drain on paper towels.

Combine the chile, soy sauce, vinegar and sugar in a bowl. Arrange the tofu on a platter. Spoon the sauce over and scatter with the scallions. Serve immediately.

PREP AHEAD

You can wrap the tofu in paper towels and leave to drain all day in the refrigerator, and the sauce can be made on the morning of serving. Fry just before serving.

THE SKINNY

The skinny soy-vinegar sauce gives healthful tofu the taste it needs.

Instant skinny snacks

We all get that moment in our day when we feel insanely famished but can't be bothered to make anything. Two hours after lunch or just before dinner are desperate hours when your blood sugar drops, and chips, cheese and other junk foods beckon. Whether it's just grazing, or arranging a little platter of tidbits for friends and family, this list is a useful reminder of the "good" snacks to have on hand when you're peckish. Most of these items keep for a long time in the fridge or pantry so stock up on your favorites for those critical hungry moments.

SNACKS FOR GRAZING, ON THE GO OR AT THE OFFICE
- dried apricots, cherries or raisins
- raw nuts
- wasabi peas
- steamed edamame with salt
- sliced apples and pears
- rice crackers
- vegetable crudités
- popcorn
- low-fat crackers, such as Ryvita
- plain bagel chips
- baked pita chips
- baked tortilla chips with fresh salsa
- pretzels with honey-mustard dip
- soy-roasted sunflower seeds or pumpkin seeds or a mix
- pickled cucumbers

MIDDLE EASTERN NIBBLES
- low-fat hummus
- baba ghanoush
- low-fat Greek-style yogurt (mixed with a little harissa or other spice)
- dukkah-spice dip with crudité and hard-cooked eggs
- warm lavash bread
- crisp baby romaine lettuce leaves
- fresh radishes and cucumbers
- pistachios in the shell
- olives
- jarred roasted peppers, mixed with harissa or chile and oil

ANTIPASTI OR TAPAS
- marinated olives
- caperberries
- canned lupuni beans
- fava beans
- sun-blushed or sun-dried tomatoes
- jarred marinated artichoke hearts
- breadsticks
- marinated boquerones
- toasted almonds or other nuts
- pickled vegetables
- Italian pickled peppers
- pickled red cherry peppers
- pickled garlic
- toasted sourdough bread rubbed with olive oil and a clove of garlic
- melon or purple figs with prosciutto or serrano ham
- low-fat tzatziki dip

SCANDINAVIAN FISH AND BREAD
- smoked mackerel or trout fillets
- gravlax or smoked salmon
- small cooked shrimp or canned crabmeat
- toasted brown, pumpernickel or rye bread
- sliced red onions
- capers
- shredded fresh horseradish or store-bought horseradish cream
- sliced cucumber
- Dijon mustard
- quartered cherry tomatoes
- sliced pickled beets
- fresh dill or scallions

Starters

Sashimi tuna with yuzu dressing

preparation time 5 minutes / freezing time 10 minutes / serves 4

If you have access to outstanding fresh fish, sashimi isn't as intimidating as one would imagine. If using tuna, choose a good-quality, deep red piece with as little marbling as possible. A sharp knife and freezing the fish for 10 minutes before preparing makes slicing very easy. Yuzu juice is a Japanese citrus juice, which is available in bottles from Japanese grocers. It tastes like a cross between grapefruit and lime and can be easily substituted with just that.

¾-pound piece of ruby-red tuna
   or sea bass, skin removed
2 scallions, finely chopped
4 handfuls mizuna
baby mustard leaves
2 tablespoons chopped chives

Yuzu dressing
½ clove garlic
3 tablespoons yuzu juice (or equal
   parts grapefruit and lime juice)
1 teaspoon soy sauce
1 teaspoon peanut oil
black pepper

Place the fish in the freezer for 10 minutes to firm up, then slice as thin as possible with a very sharp knife.

Meanwhile, make the yuzu dressing. Pound the garlic using a mortar and pestle to a paste or use the flat edge of a knife. Mix in the remaining dressing ingredients and crack some black pepper in.

Arrange the fish, scallions and greens on plates and pour on the dressing. Sprinkle with the chives.

PREP AHEAD

The fish can be sliced 4 hours ahead and stored between sheets of parchment paper in the fridge; plastic wrap isn't ideal as it makes the fish sweat.

THE SKINNY

Sashimi is about as healthy and easy as food gets. The yuzu-soy dressing has a scant amount of oil and makes a great salty-sour dipping sauce.

Tomato tartines with goat cheese and caper, mint and balsamic dressing

preparation time 20 minutes / cooking time 5 minutes / serves 4

Tartine is a gorgeous French term for an open-faced sandwich. Alongside some salad, it makes an elegant starter or lunch. Make this when tomatoes are in their summer glory and choice varieties abound.

4 thick slices sourdough bread
1 clove garlic, halved
9 ounces mixed tomatoes, such as
    cherry, yellow, zebra, green or plum
2 ounces soft goat's cheese
2 small shallots, thinly sliced

Caper, mint and balsamic dressing
3 tablespoons finely chopped mint
3 tablespoons extra virgin olive oil
2 tablespoons balsamic vinegar
1 tablespoon capers in brine, drained
    and chopped
2 teaspoons superfine sugar
sea salt
black pepper

To make the caper, mint and balsamic dressing, place all the ingredients in a small glass jar with a lid, season with sea salt and freshly ground black pepper and shake well.

Trim the bread into large squares or rectangles and toast. Rub with the garlic and season with salt and pepper. Slice the tomatoes into quarters or halves depending on their size. Spread the goat cheese on the toast, top with the tomatoes and pour the dressing over. Top with the shallots and serve.

PREP AHEAD

The dressing can be made 8 hours ahead, but assemble the tomato, cheese and bread just before eating.

THE SKINNY

Tartines make a healthful replacement for pastry, but you still get that pastry-style crunch factor. The amount of goat cheese used here is minimal but greatly contributes to the flavor.

Fresh beef and mango spring rolls

preparation time 1 hour / cooking time 10 minutes / makes 8

On a magical trip to Vietnam, I ate this surprising combination. The Vietnamese are the masters of fresh delicate food that utilizes healthy ingredients. Fruit and meat in fresh spring rolls was not a pairing I had tasted before, but the sweet mango complemented the rich beef. Pineapple and sliced cooked pork was another pairing that I tasted and it was equally good.

olive oil spray

9-ounce piece of beef tenderloin,
   trimmed of all fat

8 round rice paper wrappers
   (6 inches in diameter),
   plus extra to have as spares

1 mango, cut into ½-inch -thick pieces

2 shallots, thinly sliced

1 small handful mint leaves

1 small handful basil leaves

8 cilantro sprigs,
   about 3 inches long

1 bunch chives

sea salt

black pepper

Dipping sauce

¼ cup lime juice

2 tablespoons fish sauce

2 tablespoons water

1 thumb-sized red chile, halved,
   seeds removed and thinly sliced

1 clove garlic, finely chopped

Heat a nonstick skillet over high heat, spray with oil and season the beef with sea salt and freshly ground black pepper. Sear the meat for 2–3 minutes each side. Allow to rest for 10 minutes. Thinly slice and set aside.

Meanwhile, make the dipping sauce. Mix all the ingredients together and pour into a couple of small bowls.

Place a large kitchen towel on a work surface. Fill a wide shallow bowl with warm water. Soak a rice paper wrapper in the water for about 30 seconds. When soft and pliable, place the wrapper on the kitchen towel and wipe off the excess water with another towel. Place a small pile of beef, mango, shallot, mint, basil and cilantro at the bottom of the wrapper. Fold the sides in, then roll up tightly to enclose. Just before you finish rolling it up all the way, place a chive in the spring roll and finish rolling up. Place, seam side down, on another kitchen towel. Repeat with the remaining wrappers and filling. Throw away any wrappers that rip and start again with a fresh one. It may take a few tries to get the knack so don't get discouraged. If the wrapper is too soft, it will fall apart, and if it's too hard, it will not stick together. Practise soaking a few so you can get a feel for the right consistency.

When ready to serve, cut each spring roll in half diagonally with a very sharp knife. Serve with the dipping sauce.

PREP AHEAD

Spring rolls can be made 12 hours ahead. Line a tray with parchment paper and place spring rolls, cover with more parchment paper, then plastic wrap. This keeps them from drying out. Refrigerate until ready to serve.

THE SKINNY

Fresh Vietnamese spring rolls don't contain any oil and can be filled with all sorts of ingredients from rice noodles to chicken or shrimp. They are a tasty guilt-free treat.

Steamed asparagus with chopped egg vinaigrette

preparation time 10 minutes / cooking time 5 minutes / serves 4

Spring is asparagus's time to shine, and this ravishing sauce brings out the best in the knobbly green spears. It's based on the French ravigote dressing, which sometimes has tarragon and mustard as well.

16 thick asparagus spears, trimmed

Chopped egg vinaigrette
2 tablespoons extra virgin olive oil
1½ tablespoons red wine vinegar
1 tablespoon finely chopped flat-leaf (Italian) parsley
1 teaspoon capers in brine, drained and finely chopped
1 shallot, finely diced
1 hard-cooked egg, finely chopped
sea salt
black pepper

To make the chopped egg vinaigrette, mix all the ingredients in a small bowl with some sea salt and freshly ground black pepper. Whisk until smooth and set aside.

Steam the asparagus for 3 minutes or blanch for 2 minutes in salted boiling water. Drain and serve warm with the vinaigrette drizzled over.

PREP AHEAD

The asparagus can be blanched and rinsed in cold water 6 hours ahead and refrigerated. Warm again by submerging in boiling water for 30 seconds. The vinaigrette should be prepared only 2 hours ahead to keep the herbs green.

THE SKINNY

Steamed vegetables are a no-brainer for skinny food. A chunky vinaigrette uses less oil than mayonnaise or a cream-based sauce.

Beef carpaccio with arugula, scallion and Parmesan shavings

preparation time 20 minutes / freezing time 30 minutes / serves 4

This classic Italian starter is easy to slice if you partially freeze the meat before cutting. Chopped radicchio leaves are also good scattered over.

14-ounce piece of beef tenderloin,
   trimmed of all fat
3 tablespoons extra virgin olive oil
2 tablespoons finely chopped scallion
4 handfuls arugula leaves
2 tablespoons good-quality aged
   balsamic vinegar
2 tablespoons Parmesan shavings
1 lemon, cut into wedges
sea salt
black pepper

Heat a nonstick skillet over medium-high heat until very hot. Rub the beef with a tiny amount of the olive oil and season well with sea salt and freshly ground black pepper. Sear quickly for 1 minute each side until just browned all over. Remove, cool, then wrap in plastic wrap and place in the freezer for 30 minutes or until firm but not frozen.

Using a very sharp knife, slice the meat into ¼-inch-thick pieces or as thin as you can. You will need 3–4 slices per serving, depending on the size of the tenderloin. When the tenderloin gets too small to slice, just pound out the remaining pieces between two sheets of parchment paper and slice into similar sized pieces. Arrange the slices in a single layer on plates. Season, sprinkle on the scallion and place a handful of arugula on top of each. Drizzle with the vinegar and remaining olive oil. Top with the Parmesan shavings and serve with a lemon wedge.

PREP AHEAD

You can slice the meat 4 hours ahead, drizzle it with olive oil and refrigerate it, covered in plastic wrap. Just be sure to wrap the beef tightly to keep it from discoloring.

THE SKINNY

Carpaccio is not only delicious but is also very low in fat and high in protein. You're guaranteed to be happy and full.

Vegetable and scallion pancakes with dipping sauce

preparation time 10 minutes / cooking time 25 minutes / serves 4

These Korean-inspired pancakes are fast to whip up and don't require much oil to cook them. Serve up with a spicy green salad and use the dipping sauce to dress it.

⅔ cup self-rising flour
⅛ cup low-fat milk
3 eggs, lightly beaten
2 cups bean sprouts
6 scallions, cut into 1¼-inch lengths
1 pound sweet potato, peeled and cut
   into thin matchsticks
vegetable oil spray

Chile-soy dipping sauce
3 tablespoons rice vinegar
2 tablespoons soy sauce
1 tablespoon sesame seeds, toasted
1 red bird's eye chile, sliced
1 tablespoon superfine sugar
sea salt
black pepper

To make the chile-soy dipping sauce, combine all the ingredients in a bowl, stir and set aside.

Place the flour and a pinch of sea salt and freshly ground black pepper in a large bowl. Whisking constantly, add the milk and egg. Whisk until a smooth batter forms, then add the bean sprouts, scallions and sweet potato and gently combine. The mixture should be thick.

Heat a large nonstick skillet over medium-low heat and spray with a tiny bit of oil. Spoon ¼ cupfuls of batter into the pan to make 3–4 pancakes at a time and cook for about 4 minutes each side, making sure the sweet potato is cooked. Serve with the sauce.

PREP AHEAD

The vegetables can be chopped ahead and stored in a bowl of cold water. Drain and dry before mixing with the flour and eggs. Make the batter up to 1 hour ahead. The dipping sauce can be prepared 8 hours ahead.

THE SKINNY

Vegetable pancakes don't have to be caloric if you use a heavy nonstick skillet and oil spray, and with long, low heat you can achieve a crisp exterior.

Miso vegetable yakitori

preparation time 20 minutes / cooking time 5 minutes / serves 4

One of my favorite Japanese restaurants in London is Tosa. It's a proper yakitoria with a charcoal grill. One of their signature dishes is onion lollipops, which are easy to make, as are the two other types of skewers here. Eat as a snack or with rice.

1 red onion
4 fat scallions
1 small eggplant
8 shiitake mushrooms, stems discarded
2 tablespoons vegetable oil or oil spray
sea salt
black pepper

Miso glaze
2 tablespoons white miso
2 tablespoons mirin
1 tablespoon superfine sugar

If using wooden skewers, remember to soak them in water for 10 minutes before using. Cut the onion into 4 thick slices. Slice the white part of the scallions into 1½-inch lengths and finely chop the green part to garnish later. Cut the eggplant into 1-inch chunks.

To make the miso glaze, mix all the ingredients in a bowl and set aside.

Thread 2 mushrooms onto a skewer, with a scallion chunk in between to make 4 skewers. For the onion lollipops, run a skewer through each slice (so that the onion sits flat, like a lollipop). For the eggplant skewers, thread 3–4 chunks onto each of 4 skewers. Brush or spray all the vegetables with the oil and season with sea salt and freshly ground black pepper.

Preheat a grill pan to high. Grill the skewers for 2 minutes each side, then brush with the miso glaze. Sprinkle with the reserved chopped scallion.

PREP AHEAD

The skewers and miso glaze can be made 8 hours ahead and refrigerated. Grill just before serving.

THE SKINNY

Miso makes a tasty glaze for grilling vegetables, fish, poultry or meat. Made from fermented soybeans, it is very healthful and has only a few calories.

Steamed artichokes with lemon and oregano dipping sauce

preparation time 15 minutes / cooking time 30 minutes / serves 4

If you have a steamer or a pasta pot with a fitted insert, it's perfect for this. You want the large artichokes to steam rather than sit in water and become soggy. When they're done, dip the leaves in the sauce, then zip the leaves through your front teeth to eat. When you get to the heart (the good bit), remember to discard the fuzzy choke with a spoon. This can be removed beforehand, but it's a bit of an arduous task.

4 artichokes
1 lemon, halved

Lemon-oregano dipping sauce
3 tablespoons extra virgin olive oil
1 tablespoon chopped fresh oregano
  or 1 teaspoon dried wild oregano
1 clove garlic, bruised
1 shallot, finely chopped
finely grated zest and juice of 1 lemon
1 large pinch of chile flakes
sea salt
black pepper

Place 2–3 sturdy and heatproof mugs upside-down in the bottom of a large stockpot or deep saucepan. Pour in 3 inches water and bring to a boil. Remove the stems from the artichokes and pull off the very hard leaves at the base. Using scissors, cut the tips off all the leaves. Squeeze one half of the lemon over them. Place the artichokes, right side up, on top of the mugs, so that they will steam rather than sit in the water. Squeeze in the remaining lemon half, cover with the lid and steam for 30 minutes or until a skewer inserted into the thickest part of the artichokes withdraws easily.

Meanwhile, make the lemon-oregano dipping sauce. Whisk all the ingredients in a small bowl with some sea salt and freshly ground black pepper. Leave it to sit with the garlic, so the flavor comes through.

Pour the dressing into 4 small bowls and serve with the steamed artichokes.

PREP AHEAD

Prepare the dipping sauce a couple of hours ahead and refrigerate. Trim the artichokes 4 hours ahead but keep in some water with lemon juice added to keep the edges from blackening.

THE SKINNY

This is an easy way to prepare globe artichokes. The steaming and vinaigrette dipping sauce keep the calories and fat paltry. Apart from being delicious, they are fun to eat.

Crisp pork in lettuce cups with chile-lime dressing

preparation time 15 minutes / cooking time 10 minutes / serves 4

This speedy starter, known as **larb** in Thailand, is an impressive dish to throw together for a snack or appetizer. The pork is pan-fried until crisp, then tossed with a sweet and sour lime dressing.

2 lemongrass stalks
1 tablespoon vegetable oil
14 ounces lean ground pork
1 tablespoon grated jaggery sugar or
   light brown sugar
1 small red onion, finely diced
1 handful cilantro leaves, chopped, plus
   extra sprigs for serving
2 heads baby romaine lettuce, leaves
   separated, washed and chilled

Chile-lime dressing

¼ cup lime juice
1 tablespoon fish sauce
1 tablespoon shred jaggery or light
   brown sugar
1 clove garlic, finely chopped
1 thumb-sized red chile, seeds removed
   and finely chopped

To make the chile-lime dressing, mix all the ingredients together until the sugar has dissolved.

Remove the tough outer layers of the lemongrass until you get to the tender pale heart. Cut off and discard the green tops and trim ¾–1¼ inches off the base. Finely chop the remainder.

Heat the oil in a large wok over high heat. Add the pork and cook until crisp and brown on the bottom before breaking it up with a spoon. Add the lemongrass and cook for another 2–3 minutes or until tender. Add the sugar, stir again, then remove from the heat.

Pour the dressing over the warm pork and add the onion and cilantro. Gently stir and serve with the chilled lettuce leaves for scooping up bits.

PREP AHEAD

The pork can be made 1 day ahead and refrigerated. Reheat and pour the dressing over just before serving.

THE SKINNY

Crisp baby romaine lettuce is a fresh and clean alternative to fried wrappers to use as a base for Thai or other Asian toppings. The chile-lime dressing contains no oil and elevates the stir-fried pork.

Ceviche with arugula salad

preparation time 15 minutes / marinating time 1 hour / serves 6

The trick with ceviche or raw fish is to cut the fish into thin slices or small pieces. Technically it's raw, but it looks cooked because the citrus juice turs the fish opaque. Once it turns pearly white, drain it, then re-dress it. My friend Victoria, an amazing food writer and caterer, gave me this light and captivating recipe.

¾ pound lemon sole fillet
   (or other good-quality white fish),
   skin and bones removed
4 limes
1 shallot, finely chopped
1 tablespoon white wine vinegar
1 heaped teaspoon sea salt
1 tablespoon chopped cilantro
1 teaspoon capers in brine, drained
   and rinsed
1 tablespoon extra virgin olive oil
1 thumb-sized red chile, seeds removed
finely chopped arugula leaves, to serve
sea salt
black pepper

Slice the lemon sole into very small pieces and place in 2 separate bowls. Finely shred the zest of 1 lime, then juice it along with the other 2 limes. Cut the remaining lime into wedges.

Whisk together the shallot, vinegar, lime zest and juice and the salt. Divide the dressing between the 2 bowls of fish, cover and refrigerate for 1 hour.

Drain the fish, season with sea salt and freshly ground black pepper and toss together with the cilantro, capers, olive oil and chile. Spoon the fish onto plates. Place some arugula over the fish and serve with the lime wedges.

PREP AHEAD

The fish can be sliced 8 hours ahead and refrigerated, stored between layers of parchment paper but not marinated until 1 hour before serving, otherwise it gets tough.

THE SKINNY

With its citrus dressing, chile and capers, ceviche is very low in fat and stratospherically high in flavor.

Baked sesame shrimp with roasted chile dipping sauce

preparation time 20 minutes / cooking time 5 minutes / serves 4

Over the years I have experimented, mostly unsuccessfully, with baking Asian starters instead of frying them. This egg white and sesame seed coating was a revelation because it creates a crisp exterior that seals the shrimp to keep them juicy.

16 raw large shrimp, peeled and
   deveined with tails left on
2 egg whites
¼ cup sesame seeds, toasted
cooking oil spray
thinly sliced scallion, to serve
sea salt
black pepper

Sticky chile dipping sauce
14 tablespoons rice vinegar
6 tablespoons superfine sugar
2 tablespoons chile flakes
1 shallot, thinly sliced

Preheat the oven to 400°F.
To make the sticky chile dipping sauce, heat the vinegar and sugar with a large pinch of salt in a saucepan over medium heat. Bring to a boil, then simmer for 5 minutes or until syrupy. Remove from the heat and add the chile flakes. Set aside until cool, then add the shallot.

Butterfly the shrimp. To do this, make a deep cut down the back so they lie nearly flat. Whisk the egg white until just foamy, then dip the shrimp in the egg white, allowing the excess to drain off. Season with sea salt and freshly ground black pepper and roll in the sesame seeds. Place on a baking sheet, spray with a bit of oil and bake for 5 minutes or until they turn opaque and start to curl a bit. Serve warm, garnished with the scallion, with the dipping sauce on the side.

PREP AHEAD

The shrimp can be coated 2 hours before cooking and refrigerated, stored between layers of parchment paper, then wrapped in plastic wrap. The dipping sauce can be made 1 day ahead, but don't add the shallots until closer to serving.

THE SKINNY

The egg white and sesame coating seals in the shrimp and crisps while it bakes. No deep-fryers in sight!

Stromboli salad with tomato, boquerones and oregano

preparation time 10 minutes / cooking time 5 minutes / serves 4

I remember when my family and I rented a house in Palermo, Sicily, and spent a day visiting the nearby Aeolian Islands. They are best known for their tiny capers, grown in the arid volcanic soil, and locally fished anchovies. The snowy-white fillets are marinated in vinegar and served with only a splash of olive oil. Fortunately, they export them so we can experience the same pleasures back home. I usually drain them from the oil they're packed in and give them a gentle rinse before using.

1 cup sourdough bread cubes

2 tablespoons extra virgin olive oil

6 tomatoes, such as small beefsteak, plum or baby romas, cut into small chunks

16 boquerones

1 tablespoon chopped oregano

2 small shallots, thinly sliced

1 tablespoon small capers in brine, drained and rinsed

1 tablespoon red wine vinegar

sea salt

black pepper

Preheat the oven to 400°F. Toss the bread cubes with 1 tablespoon of the olive oil and some sea salt and freshly ground black pepper. Bake for 5–6 minutes or until golden. Remove and allow to cool.

Combine the tomatoes, boquerones, croutons, oregano, shallots and capers in a big bowl. Just before serving, drizzle in the vinegar and remaining olive oil and season.
Mix well and serve.

PREP AHEAD

The croutons can be prepared 1 day ahead and stored in an airtight container. Chop up all the ingredients a couple of hours ahead but don't toss together until serving.

THE SKINNY

Pungent oregano and a tangy splash of red wine vinegar add flavor while keeping the oil quantity low. Marinated anchovies are low in fat but high in protein, making the salad more substantial.

Spicy scallops with avocado and mango salsa

preparation time 15 minutes / cooking time 5 minutes / serves 4

Large shrimp can be used here, so feel free to substitute. The trick to getting a good sear on scallops is to get the skillet smoking hot. Heavy old-fashioned cast iron skillets are ideal but use the best one you have.

12 scallops, trimmed and cleaned
1 teaspoon olive oil
1 teaspoon mild ground chile pepper
   or smoked paprika
1 lime, cut into wedges

Avocado and mango salsa
1 avocado, diced
1 mango, diced
1 small red onion, finely diced
2 tablespoons chopped cilantro
finely grated zest and juice of 1 lime
2 teaspoons chipotle hot pepper sauce or
   ¼ teaspoon regular hot pepper sauce
sea salt
black pepper

To make the avocado and mango salsa, mix the ingredients in a small bowl. Season with sea salt and freshly ground black pepper and set aside.

Rub the scallops with the oil and chile powder and season well.

When you're ready to eat, divide the salsa among 4 plates. Heat a cast iron skillet over high heat until very hot. Sear the scallops for about 1 minute each side; let them get crisp and browned before you turn them. You will need to sear them in two batches so that the skillet is not overcrowded. Top each plate with the scallops and a lime wedge and serve immediately.

PREP AHEAD

The whole dish may be prepped ahead but no more than an hour before serving. Cover with plastic wrap close to the surface to prevent the avocado from browning.

THE SKINNY

Avocado is considered high in fat but it's the good type, monounsaturated. It pairs very well with scallops. The salsa enhances the taste and keeps the dish skinny.

Salads for Dinner
or On The Side

Turkish bulgur salad

preparation time 30 minutes / serves 4–6

A Turkish au pair in my neighborhood gave me this recipe and it's one of my favorite salads. It keeps for up to 4 days refrigerated, making it handy for lunch boxes or as an impromptu healthy meal alongside a broiled piece of meat. Traditionally, a Turkish pepper paste is used in place of the tomato paste but it's not that easy to get hold of. If you have access to a Turkish food store, sample the chile powders and pastes — it will open a new world for you.

2¼ cups fine bulgur

2 cups boiling water

12 scallions, thinly sliced

4 plum tomatoes, seeds removed and diced

1 small cucumber, seeds removed and diced

juice of 4 limes

1 small handful flat-leaf (Italian) parsley, chopped

1 small handful mint leaves, chopped

¼ extra virgin olive oil

3 tablespoons tomato paste

1 tablespoon pomegranate molasses (optional)

1 teaspoon mild ground chile pepper, or to taste

2 teaspoons sea salt

Place the bulgur in a large bowl and cover with the water. Allow to stand for 10 minutes, then fluff up with a fork. Add the remaining ingredients and stir together. Serve at room temperature or chilled.

PREP AHEAD

The entire salad can be made, covered and refrigerated for up to 4 days.

THE SKINNY

Bulgur is much healthier than couscous because of its high fiber content; the wheat is cracked, rather than finely milled, and sweeps your gut clean. It creates a textural base for healthy salads. If making ahead, stir in the herbs just before serving.

Roasted eggplant with goat cheese, crisp flat bread and mint-chile dressing

preparation time 15 minutes / cooking time 25 minutes / serves 4

Toasty chunks of roasted eggplant are tossed in a minty balsamic vinaigrette with crisp flat bread, a sprinkle of goat's cheese and some spicy arugula. Middle East meets West in this luscious mix. Pomegranate seeds are also nice sprinkled on top.

2 eggplants
1 tablespoon extra virgin olive oil
2 pieces lavash bread or pita bread
6 ounces mixed red and yellow cherry
   tomatoes
4 large handfuls arugula
2 shallots, thinly sliced
2 ounces hard goat cheese, crumbled
sea salt
black pepper

Mint-chile dressing
3 tablespoons balsamic vinegar
2 tablespoons extra virgin olive oil
1 large handful mint leaves,
   finely chopped
1 thumb-sized red chile, seeds removed
   and finely chopped
1 shallot, finely diced

Preheat the oven to 400°F. Cut the eggplants into 1¼-inch chunks. Drizzle with the olive oil and season with sea salt and freshly ground black pepper. Arrange on a baking sheet and roast for 25 minutes or until browned.

Rip the flat bread into pieces and place on a baking sheet. Just as the eggplant is nearly ready, pop the flat bread into the oven and bake for 8 minutes, then remove and place in a bowl.

To make the mint-chile dressing, mix all the ingredients together in a small bowl and season.

Toss about one-third of the dressing with the eggplant and save the rest to pour over the salad. Arrange the tomatoes, arugula, shallot, dressed eggplant and crisp flat bread on a large platter. Pour the reserved dressing over and scatter the goat cheese on top.

PREP AHEAD

The dressing, roasted eggplant and crisp bread can all be prepared on the morning of serving. Reheat the eggplant in a nonstick skillet over gentle heat.

THE SKINNY

Roasting eggplant uses much less oil than pan-frying and you get a crisper result. Only a small amount of goat cheese is used but you still get to enjoy the cheesy taste.

Baby greens salad with roasted beets, sugared almonds and crisp prosciutto

preparation time 20 minutes / cooking time 35 minutes / serves 4

It's the extra bits you add to a salad that make it special. Sugared almonds and crisp bits of serrano ham raise the bar for this roasted beets and greens salad. If you have access to Marcona almonds from Spain, then use them. They're starting to appear in many supermarkets and are considered the best almonds in the world.

4–5 baby beets, scrubbed and trimmed
1 teaspoon extra virgin olive oil
2 slices serrano ham or prosciutto
4 handfuls mixed baby lettuce leaves
1 head red Belgian endive, leaves
    separated
sea salt
black pepper

Sugared almonds

3 tablespoons blanched almonds,
    roughly chopped
1 tablespoon honey
1 teaspoon extra virgin olive oil
1 tablespoon superfine sugar

Dressing

1 tablespoon sherry vinegar
2½ tablespoons extra virgin olive oil
1 teaspoon Dijon mustard

Preheat the oven to 350°F. Cut the beets into quarters and place on a baking sheet. Drizzle with the olive oil and season with sea salt and freshly ground black pepper. Roast for 25 minutes or until tender and caramelized.

To make the sugared almonds, place the almonds on a baking sheet lined with parchment paper. Drizzle with the honey and olive oil, sprinkle with the sugar and season with salt. Stir to evenly coat, then bake for 10 minutes or until golden. Remove and allow to cool.

Heat a nonstick skillet over medium–high heat and cook the prosciutto for 1 minute each side or until crisp. Cool and break into pieces.

To make the dressing, place all the ingredients in a small glass jar with a lid, season and shake well.

Place the leaves on plates or in a big bowl. Arrange the beets, crisp ham and sugared almonds on top. Drizzle with the dressing and serve.

PREP AHEAD

The nuts, dressing and beets can all be made 1 day ahead and the salad assembled just before eating.

THE SKINNY

Nuts, ham, salami and cheese make salads infinitely more appealing but obviously they are higher on the fat scale. By using just a little, you still get the taste and texture but not so many calories.

Turkey and watercress salad with poppyseed vinaigrette

preparation time 10 minutes / serves 4

This has everything you want in a big salad: rainbow-coloured veggies, zingy dressing and some sustenance to keep you full. As an added bonus, it also contains more than three of your five a day. Use a julienne tool or hand-held mandolin to easily cut the carrots. Watercress is a little more peppery than spinach but you can use either.

5 ounces picked watercress, roughly chopped
1 red bell pepper, cut into matchsticks
2 large carrots, cut into matchsticks
2 tablespoons crumbled feta cheese
10 ounces roast turkey meat, shredded or sliced

Poppyseed vinaigrette
2 small shallots, finely chopped
3 tablespoons honey
2 tablespoons apple cider vinegar
2 tablespoons vegetable oil
2 teaspoons Dijon mustard
2 teaspoons poppyseeds
sea salt
black pepper

To make the poppyseed vinaigrette, place all the ingredients in a blender except the poppyseeds. Blend well and add some sea salt and freshly ground black pepper. Transfer to a bowl and stir in the poppyseeds.

Layer the watercress, bell peppers, carrots, feta in a large shallow bowl. Top with the turkey. Cover and refrigerate until using. Pour over enough dressing to coat the salad just before serving.

PREP AHEAD

The chopped ingredients will keep refrigerated for 2 days but dress just before serving.

THE SKINNY

This is another great "packed lunch" salad that will keep for days. The dressing uses very little oil and the flavor comes from the honey, mustard and lemon juice.

Crab, spinach and avocado salad with hot pepper-lime dressing

preparation time 10 minutes / cooking time 5 minutes / serves 4

Who doesn't adore fresh crab? Briny white flakes that smell like the sea is my idea of nirvana. But, if it's not available or in season, canned white crabmeat is better than you think. It's comparable to good canned tuna and much easier on the budget. Although crab doesn't need much company to make it taste good, a hot pepper sauce–spiked dressing and crisp bread crumbs make this spinach salad a step up from the ordinary.

2 handfuls chunky fresh bread crumbs
olive oil spray
5 ounces baby spinach
1 avocado, cut into chunk
8 ounces cherry tomatoes, halved
4 scallions, thinly sliced
4 ounces crabmeat
sea salt
black pepper

Hot pepper–lime dressing
juice of 2 limes
3 tablespoons extra virgin olive oil
1 tablespoon red wine vinegar
1 teaspoon hot pepper sauce
1 tablespoon honey

Preheat the oven to 400°F. Spread the bread crumbs evenly on a baking sheet. Spray with a little olive oil and season with sea salt and freshly ground black pepper. Bake for 5 minutes or until golden and crisp.

Arrange the spinach, avocado, tomatoes, scallions and crabmeat on a platter.

To make the hot-pepper-lime dressing, mix all the ingredients together in a small bowl and season. Pour over enough dressing to coat the salad and, when ready to eat, scatter the crisp bread crumbs on top.

PREP AHEAD

The crisp bread crumbs and dressing can be made 1 day ahead and the salad can be made and refrigerated 4 hours ahead. Dress and scatter the bread crumbs on top just before serving.

THE SKINNY

Croutons or crisp bread crumbs won't be so caloric if you use an olive oil spray. The dressing relies more on lime juice than oil, keeping it skinny.

Beet, pea and feta salad with dill and honey-mustard vinaigrette

preparation time 10 minutes / cooking time 20 minutes / serves 4

This fetching green and purple vegetable salad is tossed with an apple cider vinegar–based dressing and topped with a whisper of salty feta cheese. It's satisfying on its own, or great alongside broiled lamb or steak.

4 beets, scrubbed and trimmed
½ pound sugar snap peas
3½ ounces fresh or frozen shelled peas
1 tabelspoon chopped dill
1 ounce feta cheese, crumbled

Honey-mustard vinaigrette
2 tablespoons apple cider vinegar
2 tablespoons extra virgin olive oil
1 tablespoon whole-grain mustard
2 teaspoons honey
sea salt
black pepper

Place the beets in a large saucepan of lightly salted water and bring to a boil. Reduce the heat to medium and simmer for 20–25 minutes or until tender when pierced with the tip of a knife. Drain the beets and, when cool enough to handle, cut into 1¼-inch cubes and place in a bowl.

Meanwhile, make the honey-mustard vinaigrette. Place all the ingredients in a small glass jar with a lid, season with sea salt and freshly ground black pepper and shake well. Pour half over the warm beets and mix well.

Slice the sugar snaps in half lengthwise. Blanch them along with the peas for 1 minute in lightly salted boiling water. Rinse in cold water, drain well and add to the beets along with the dill.

Pour the remaining dressing over and scatter with the feta. Don't stir too much because the beets tend to turn everything purple — just scoop up and serve.

PREP AHEAD

The vegetables and dressing can be prepared 1 day ahead and refrigerated separately. Mix together before serving.

THE SKINNY

The small amount of feta cheese injects a salty taste but not a huge amount of calories. If you want to make this more substantial, eat with smoked fish or broiled meat.

Vietnamese chicken salad

preparation time 10 minutes / cooking time 20 minutes / serves 4

This is a very popular street-food dish in Vietnam. The Vietnamese boil an entire chicken, pick the bones clean, then toss the warm meat with a lime-chile dressing and chopped peanuts. Poaching transforms the chicken into velvety shreds. When dressed warm with the sweet and sour lime dressing there is only one word to describe it: unbelievable. I've taken a short cut by using chicken breasts, which are easier than using a whole bird. You could even use a warm rotisserie chicken from the supermarket.

3 small boneless, skin-on chicken breast
   halves
2 small cucumbers
1 small red onion, halved
   and thinly sliced
1 large handful basil leaves
1 large handful mint leaves
1 large handful cilantro leaves
1 thumb-sized red chile, seeds removed
   and thinly sliced
2 tablespoons roasted peanuts, chopped

Lime dressing
juice of 3 limes
1 clove garlic, crushed through a press
1 tablespoon fish sauce
1 tablespoon light brown sugar

Bring a large saucepan of water to a boil. Add the chicken breasts, cover with a lid, turn off the heat and leave on the stove for 20 minutes. Remove the chicken, discard the skin and carefully shred the meat into a bowl.

Meanwhile, make the lime dressing. Mix all the ingredients together until the sugar has dissolved.

Use a vegetable peeler to peel the cucumber into ribbons. Add to the chicken. Add the onion, herbs, chile and dressing and gently toss to combine. Serve scattered with the peanuts.

PREP AHEAD
Poach the chicken and make the dressing 8 hours ahead and refrigerate. Gently reheat the chicken to serve.

THE SKINNY
Southeast Asian dressings are perfect because they don't involve a drop of oil. Poaching is brilliant because meat stays moist and, again, no oil is required.

Brown rice salad with poached chicken, broccoli and miso dressing

preparation time 15 minutes / cooking time 20 minutes / serves 4–6

Although this one-dish salad sounds too chaste to be good, it has remarkable flavor and texture. The punchy miso-mirin dressing is a pure hit of Japanese taste, while the green vegetables add crunch and goodness. Brown basmati is a little chewier than white so use whichever you prefer. Sesame seeds or chile powder are nice sprinkled over as well.

1 cup brown basmati rice

4 cups chicken broth
   or water

3 small boneless, skinless chicken breast
   halves

½ pound broccoli, cut into small florets

4 ounces frozen shelled edamame

2 celery ribs, from the heart,
   thinly sliced

6 scallions, very thinly sliced on the
   diagonal

Miso dressing

2 tablespoons rice vinegar

2 tablespoons mirin

1 tablespoon red miso

2 teaspoons finely grated fresh ginger

Place the rice in a small saucepan, add enough water to cover by 2½ inches and bring to a boil. Reduce the heat to medium-low and simmer for 15–20 minutes or until al dente. Drain and keep warm.

While the rice is cooking, place the broth or water in a saucepan and bring to a boil. Add the chicken breasts, cover with a lid, turn off the heat and leave to sit for 20 minutes. Remove the chicken and cut into slices.

Blanch the broccoli and edamame in salted boiling water, drain and rinse under cold water.

To make the miso dressing, mix all the ingredients together in a small bowl. Thin with a little water if it's too thick.

Spread the rice on a platter and top with the chicken and all the vegetables. Pour the dressing over and top with the scallions

PREP AHEAD

The entire salad can be prepared 1 day ahead and refrigerated but not assembled until serving.

THE SKINNY

Miso is a star dressing ingredient as it has so much flavor and no oil is needed; the vinegar and mirin thin and balance out its intense saltiness. Use red or yellow miso in this dish for the best results.

Latin palm heart salad with orange, shrimp and avocado

preparation time 20 minutes / serves 4

Hearts of palm glam up any leaves with their artichoke like flavor. They're particularly good in Latin or Italian salads with a bit of avocado. Store a few cans in your cupboard for an instant starter or special side salad. Most supermarkets sell them in the canned vegetable aisle.

2 large navel oranges
1 bunch watercress, leaves picked
14-ounce can hearts of palm, drained and sliced
1 avocado, chopped into 1¼-inch pieces
16 cooked shrimp, peeled and deveined
4 scallions, chopped

Dressing
2 tablespoons lime juice
2 tablespoons vegetable oil
2 tablespoons honey
1 tablespoon red wine vinegar
1 teaspoon finely chopped cilantro
sea salt
black pepper

Use a sharp knife to cut the peel off the oranges, then cut each lengthwise into 4 slices. Drain on paper towels. Place the watercress, hearts of palm, avocado, shrimp, scallions and orange in a large bowl or on a platter.

To make the dressing, place all the ingredients in a small glass jar with a lid, season with sea salt and freshly ground black pepper and shake well. Pour over the salad just before serving.

PREP AHEAD

The dressing can be made in the morning and the salad can be chopped up a couple of hours in advance. If doing so, toss the avocado with a little lemon or lime juice to keep it from discoloring.

THE SKINNY

Shrimp are low in calories and full of protein, making them ideal to beef up a salad. Keep a bag of peeled cooked shrimp on hand in your freezer to use as a quick addition to salads.

Puy lentil salad with walnuts, apple and blue cheese vinaigrette

preparation time 30 minutes / cooking time 25 minutes / serves 4

Walnuts, blue cheese and apple go together, no doubt about it. Whether on their own, or mixed with lentils or Belgian endive, it's a winning salty, nutty and tart trio. Only a small amount of the cheese is mixed into the vinaigrette, giving you all the taste but not huge amounts of fat.

1⅛ cups Puy (French) lentils
4 cups chicken broth
  or water
1 celery heart, finely chopped
1 Granny Smith apple, peeled, cored
  and roughly chopped
2 shallots, finely diced
¼ cup walnuts, toasted
  and chopped
2 tablespoons finely chopped flat-leaf
  (Italian) parsley

Blue cheese vinaigrette
2 tablespoons extra virgin olive oil
  or walnut oil
2 tablespoons red wine vinegar
1 tablespoon crumbled strong blue
  cheese, such as Roquefort
1 teaspoon Dijon mustard
1 clove garlic, bruised
sea salt
black pepper

Place the lentils and stock or water in a large saucepan and bring to a boil. Reduce the heat to low and simmer for 20–25 minutes or until al dente. Drain and pour into a bowl. Add the celery, apple, shallots, walnuts and parsley.

To make the blue cheese vinaigrette, place all the ingredients in a small glass jar with a lid, season with sea salt and freshly ground black pepper and shake well. Remove the just before serving. Pour the dressing over the salad and toss well.

PREP AHEAD

This can be made in full and kept covered and refrigerated for 2–3 days, but hold back the parsley until serving.

THE SKINNY

Blue cheese is strong in taste, so only a little is needed to make the dressing come to life.

Baby greens with goat cheese, dried cherries and sugared hazelnuts

preparation time 15 minutes / cooking time 5 minutes / serves 4

Walnut oil and fruit vinegar make dreamy dressings for baby salad greens. Slender green beans, sugared nuts and goat cheese get tossed along with it for a special side salad or starter. Always remember to keep hazelnut or walnut oils in the refrigerator because they go off very quickly if not kept chilled.

¼ pound thin green beans trimmed (if big, halve lengthwise)
5 ounces mixed baby salad greens (mesclun)
2 tablespoons dried cherries, roughly chopped
5 scallions, sliced
2 ounces hard goat cheese, crumbled

Raspberry and nut-oil dressing
1 tablespoon raspberry or balsamic vinegar
3 tablespoons hazelnut or walnut oil
1 teaspoon Dijon mustard
1 clove garlic, bruised
sea salt
black pepper

Sugared hazelnuts
3 tablespoons hazelnuts, halved or roughly chopped
1 heaped tablespoon confectioners' sugar
sea salt

To make the sugared hazelnuts, preheat the oven to 350°F. Rinse the hazelnuts in water and toss with the confectioners' sugar and a little sea salt. Spread over an oiled baking sheet and bake for 5 minutes or until crisp. Scrape off the sheet and set aside to cool.

Meanwhile, blanch the green beans for 1 minute in salted boiling water, drain, rinse in cold water and dry. Place in a large bowl and add the salad greens, cherries, scallions and sugared hazelnuts.

To make the raspberry nut-oil dressing, place all the ingredients in a small glass jar with a lid, season with sea salt and freshly ground black pepper and shake well.

Pour enough dressing over the salad to coat and scatter over the goat cheese on top.

PREP AHEAD

The nuts, blanched beans and dressing can be made 1 day ahead and refrigerated separately.

THE SKINNY

The tiny quantity of nuts keeps the calories down but makes the salad a bit more special. You could also add broiled sliced lean steak or broil the goat cheese on a slice of toasted baguette to make it more substantial.

Potato and smoked trout salad with capers and whole-grain mustard

preparation time 20 minutes / cooking time 10 minutes / serves 4

Here is an inspired way to get your omega-3 and -6 fatty acid intake. Smoked fish such as trout and mackerel are "super" or "power" foods because they are high in these vital oils

- 1 ¾ pounds red-skinned potatoes
- 1 tablespoon red wine vinegar
- 2 teaspoons finely chopped dill
- 1 tablespoon baby capers in brine, drained and rinsed
- 1 small red onion, thinly sliced into half moons
- 4 handfuls picked watercress
- 6 ounces smoked trout or mackerel fillets, skin and bones removed, flesh broken into chunks
- sea salt
- black pepper

Dressing
- 2 tablespoons whole-grain mustard
- 2 tablespoons red wine vinegar
- 2 tablespoons extra virgin olive oil
- 1 teaspoon superfine sugar

Place the potatoes in a saucepan of lightly salted water and bring to a boil. Simmer for 10 minutes or until tender when pierced with the tip of a knife, then drain. When cool enough to handle, peel and cut into thick slices. Place in a bowl and toss with the vinegar and some sea salt and freshly ground black pepper.

To make the dressing, mix all the ingredients together in a small bowl. Pour over the potatoes and add the dill, capers and onion. Arrange the salad on plates with a handful of the watercress, then top with the smoked trout.

PREP AHEAD

This can be made 1 day ahead; add the toppings just before serving.

THE SKINNY

Smoked fish such as trout and mackerel are powerhouses for health and are a great protein to add to salads. Dress the potato salad while warm to let the flavors soak in.

Chopped tarragon, bacon and chicken salad

preparation time 15 minutes / cooking time 5 minutes / serves 4

~~~~~~

If you have leftover chicken, this salad tossed in a French vinaigrette is a clever solution. Alternatively, you can buy a rotisserie chicken and shred the meat. It's a bit like a Cobb salad but all mixed together.

3 lean bacon slices
1 large avocado, cut into small chunks
4 ounces broiled or poached chicken, shredded
6 ounces cherry tomatoes, halved
1 celery heart, thinly sliced
2 teaspoons chopped tarragon
5 scallions, thinly sliced
¾ cup shelled fresh or frozen peas, blanched

Dressing
3 tablespoons extra virgin olive oil
2 tablespoons white balsamic or white wine vinegar
1 tablespoon Dijon mustard
pinch of sugar
sea salt

Heat a nonstick skillet over medium-high heat until very hot. Add the bacon and cook until golden and crisp. Remove and drain on paper towels. It should be crisp enough to crumble easily.

To make the dressing, mix all the ingredients with a pinch of sea salt in a small bowl.

Place the avocado, chicken, tomato, celery, tarragon, scallions, peas and bacon in a large bowl. Pour over the dressing and toss gently to combine.

. . . .

PREP AHEAD

The salad can be made 4 hours ahead, dressed and refrigerated.

THE SKINNY

Bacon is high on the fat scale so the idea is to just have a little taste of it. Chicken keeps you full, making this a healthy one-dish meal that won't leave you hankering for a snack a few hours later.

Sushi salad with seared tuna, avocado and rice wine dressing

preparation time 20 minutes / cooking time 15 minutes / serves 4

If you love sushi but can't be bothered rolling it, this is the ticket. This past year I finally relented and bought a rice cooker and it's one appliance that never gathers dust. The rice always comes out perfect and you don't need to babysit it while cooking.

1 ⅓ cups sushi rice, rinsed
   3 times until the water runs clear
1⅓ cups water
⅓ cup rice vinegar
2 tablespoons superfine sugar
1 pound 2 ounces tuna fillet
   or 2 thick tuna steaks
cooking oil spray
1 sheet nori (seaweed), shredded
1 avocado, sliced
1 small red onion, thinly sliced
   into half moons
1 tablespoon black or white sesame
   seeds, toasted
sea salt
black pepper

Place the rice and water in a saucepan, cover and bring to a boil. Reduce the heat to low and simmer for 12 minutes or until the water is absorbed. Remove from the heat and leave covered for 10 minutes.

Place the vinegar, sugar and a pinch of salt in a small saucepan over medium heat, stirring to dissolve the sugar. Remove from the heat.

Season the tuna liberally with freshly ground black pepper, spray with a little oil and sear in a nonstick skillet over very high heat for 1 minute each side. Remove and allow to cool.

Spread the hot rice in a large glass baking dish or plastic tray. Drizzle two-thirds of the rice vinegar dressing over and gently mix using a spatula. Add the shredded nori and mix again. Spoon the rice onto plates.

Slice the tuna and place over each serving. Add the avocado and onion and sprinkle with the sesame seeds. Serve with a bowl of the remaining rice vinegar dressing to pass around.

PREP AHEAD

Sushi rice doesn't taste good refrigerated so it's better to cool it quickly and leave it covered at room temperature. Make it 2 hours ahead. The fish can be seared and sliced about 8 hours ahead and refrigerated.

THE SKINNY

Seared fish and rice is the perfect one-dish meal and with all of the extra toppings you won't feel deprived.

Tuna pasta salad with peppadews, basil and balsamic dressing

preparation time 20 minutes / cooking time 10 minutes / serves 4

There isn't a drop of mayonnaise in sight here. Frankly, it's just not needed with all the flavor components such as pickled peppers, capers and sweet balsamic dressing. Orecchiette is great in pasta salads because of its thickness. They won't go soggy and their little pockets tuck in all the tasty bits. Peppadews are little red cherry peppers that are pickled. They are similar to Italian pepperoncini but less spicy. Sold all over the world in supermarkets, they perk up salads and burgers and they're delicious as part of an antipasti platter.

12 ounces orecchiette (little ears) pasta
6½ ounces canned tuna in brine, drained
  and flaked
1 tablespoon baby capers, drained and
  rinsed
1 celery heart, chopped
1 small red onion, finely diced
2 tablespoons finely chopped basil
15 pickled peppadews peppers, chopped
arugula leaves and halved cherry
  tomatoes, to serve (optional)

Balsamic dressing
3 tablespoons balsamic vinegar
3 tablespoons extra virgin olive oil
1 teaspoon superfine sugar
sea salt
black pepper

Cook the pasta in salted boiling water for 10 minutes or until al dente. Drain, rinse in cold water and drain again. Pour into a large bowl and add the tuna, capers, celery, onion, basil and peppadews.

To make the balsamic dressing, place all the ingredients in a small glass jar with a lid, season with sea salt and freshly ground black pepper and shake well.

Pour over the pasta and mix well. Add the arugula and cherry tomatoes to up the vegetable factor if you like.

PREP AHEAD

This salad will keep for 3 days, covered in the refrigerator. You may want to add the arugula and tomatoes a bit later to keep them fresher.

THE SKINNY

With the exception of the celery and basil, nearly all the ingredients here are pantry staples. It's wise to have a well-stocked pantry so you can make skinny salads on the fly. The balsamic dressing pumps up the taste without mayonnaise or excess oil.

Rice noodle salad with turkey, carrot and lime-chile dressing

preparation time 20 minutes / cooking time 10 minutes / serves 4

This makes a great cold packed lunch for work, as the ingredients stand up well to the dressing for a long time. Chicken breast can be used in place of the turkey, just pulse it in the food processor until minced.

4 ounces dried thin rice noodles
1 thumb-sized red chile, seeds removed
   and cut into thin slices
2 carrots, shredded
1 small red onion, thinly sliced
   into half moons
1 handful cilantro leaves, roughly
   chopped
1 handful mint leaves, roughly chopped
cooking oil spray
1 pound 2 ounces ground turkey

Lime-chile dressing
2 tablespoons fish sauce
2 tablespoons light brown sugar
juice of 4 small limes
1 clove garlic, crushed through a press

Pour boiling water over the noodles and allow to sit for 5 minutes. Drain, rinse under cold water and place in a large bowl, along with the chile, carrots, onion and herbs.

To make the lime-chile dressing, mix all the ingredients together.

Heat a nonstick skillet or wok over high heat until extremely hot. Lightly coat with oil and cook the ground turkey until it is nicely browned, then break into chunks. Add to the noodle mixture, pour the dressing over the salad and mix well.

PREP AHEAD

The entire salad can be prepared 1 day ahead, covered and refrigerated.

THE SKINNY

Ground turkey is much lower in fat than pork, which is normally used in a salad such as this. With virtuous meat and a tasty oil-free dressing, this makes a spectacular lean lunch.

Beef, radicchio and mushroom salad with lemon-Parmesan dressing

preparation time 20 minutes / cooking time 10 minutes / resting time 10 minutes / serves 4

Bitter radicchio and crisp celery join forces with velvety beef and mushrooms, and it all gets tossed in a sharp lemon-parmesan dressing.

6 ounces button mushrooms, very thinly sliced

1 celery heart, very thinly sliced

2 large handfuls radicchio or 1 small head red Belgian endive, sliced

¼ pound cherry tomatoes, halved

½ beef tenderloin or sirloin steak, trimmed of all fat

1 teaspoon extra virgin olive oil

sea salt

black pepper

Lemon-Parmesan dressing

3 tablespoons extra virgin olive oil

2 tablespoons finely grated Parmesan

2 teaspoons superfine sugar

finely grated zest and juice of 2 lemons

1 clove garlic, bruised

Place the mushrooms, celery, radicchio and tomatoes in a bowl. Rub the beef with the olive oil and season with sea salt and freshly ground black pepper.

Heat a nonstick skillet over very high heat until very hot and sear the beef for about 2 minutes each side. Remove and let sit for 10 minutes, then thinly slice. Add to the bowl of salad.

To make the dressing, place all the ingredients in a small glass jar with a lid, season with sea salt and freshly ground black pepper and shake well. Keep the garlic back when pouring the dressing over the salad. Toss gently and serve.

PREP AHEAD

Broil and slice the steak and make the dressing 1 day ahead, but chop the other ingredients a couple of hours in advance and mix just before serving.

THE SKINNY

Beef satiates you like no other protein. It doesn't have to be caloric if you buy a lean cut such as sirloin or tenderloin. Trim any excess fat before slicing. Only a small amount of Parmesan is used but the nutty taste still comes through the dressing.

Iceberg wedges with Japanese ginger-onion dressing

preparation time 15 minutes / serves 4

Whenever I eat at a Japanese restaurant I always order this type of salad. For years I have been messing about trying to recreate the ginger dressing. After many revisions I think this is pretty close. It looks like a long list of ingredients but it all goes in the blender and gets pureed. Make as a starter or side or transform it into a one-dish meal with some grilled steak or tuna.

1 head iceberg lettuce or 4 baby gem
   lettuces, halved
2 beefsteak tomatoes, cut into wedges
2 carrots, shredded
1 small cucumber, thinly sliced

Japanese ginger-onion dressing

2 tablespoons rice vinegar
2 tablespoons soy sauce
2 tablespoons white sugar
1 tablespoon tomato paste
1 tablespoon vegetable oil
1 tablespoon water
2 teaspoons chopped fresh ginger
1 tablespoon finely chopped
   white onion
½ celery rib, chopped

To make the Japanese ginger-onion dressing, place all the ingredients in a blender or food processor and process until smooth, then pour into a small pitcher.

Cut the lettuce into 4 wedges and remove any soft outer leaves. Place a wedge on each plate. Arrange the tomatoes, carrots and cucumber alongside. Just before serving, drizzle with enough dressing to coat the salad.

PREP AHEAD

The dressing can be made 1 day ahead, but keep it in a glass jar with a lid so you can shake it again before pouring.

THE SKINNY

This ginger and wine vinegar dressing has so much punch but only 1 tablespoon of oil. You certainly won't feel like you're missing out.

Soups for
Dinner or To Start

Shabu shabu beef and vegetable soup

preparation time 10 minutes / freezing time 15 minutes / cooking time 10 minutes / serves 4

Traditionally this soup is served in a hotpot and the various vegetables, meat and noodles are dipped into the hot broth, then eaten with soy or sesame sauces. I have taken great liberties in combining the beef and vegetables into the soup base. You can add cooked udon noodles to the finished soup, but the soup is already quite satisfying for such a simple combination.

6 ounces beef tenderloin or sirloin
   steak, trimmed of all fat
4 cups beef, chicken
   or vegetable broth
3 tablespoons ponzu sauce
3 tablespoons mirin
1 large onion, halved and thinly sliced
2 small carrots, peeled and cut
   into ¾ inch pieces
2 baby leeks, white part only,
   thinly sliced
3 ounces savoy cabbage,
   finely shredded
2 scallions, thinly sliced
1 tablespoon sesame seeds, toasted

Place the beef in the freezer for 15 minutes or longer if you can. You just want it firm but not frozen. When firm, use your sharpest knife to cut it into very thin slices and set aside. You can also ask a butcher to do this for you, or Japanese supermarkets sell beef already sliced.
   Bring the broth to a simmer in a saucepan and pour in the ponzu and mirin. Add the onion, carrots, leeks and cabbage and simmer for 7–8 minutes or until tender but still firm. Divide the beef among serving bowls, pour in the soup and serve immediately, sprinkled with scallions and sesame seeds.

PREP AHEAD

This soup is best made just before serving so the vegetables remain fresh and al dente.

THE SKINNY

Poaching all the ingredients requires no oil at all and the ponzu and mirin add immense flavor to the broth.

Quick shrimp noodle soup with fresh herbs

preparation time 15 minutes / cooking time 10 minutes / serves 4

Pho is the heart-and-soul noodle soup of Vietnam. You'll find a street vendor on practically every corner selling it with people hunched over, slurping up noodles. Here it's made with shrimp, but you can use chopped beef, pork or chicken. Just add your favorite meat to the broth base, which is aromatic with hints of ginger, star anise and cinnamon. The fresh herbs and chile sauce make it an eating experience and no other dishes are needed. Fresh bean sprouts are also a nice addition and give it a little crunch.

7 ounces dried thick rice noodles
4 cups chicken or vegetable broth
1 tablespoon fish sauce
juice of 2 limes
2-inch piece of fresh gingert, cut into
  slices
1 cinnamon stick
2 star anise
pinch of sugar
16 raw shrimp, peeled and deveined with
  tails left on
6 scallions, thinly sliced
2 handfuls basil leaves
2 handfuls mint leaves
2 handfuls cilantro leaves
Vietnamese or Chinese chile sauce,
  to serve

Cook the noodles in a saucepan of boiling water for 3–5 minutes or until al dente and drain. Divide among bowls.

Meanwhile, heat the stock in a saucepan and add the fish sauce, lime juice, ginger, cinnamon, star anise and sugar. Bring to a boil, then add the shrimp and simmer gently for 2 minutes.

Divide the shrimp among the bowls and pour the soup over the top. Top with the scallions and herbs. Serve with the chile sauce on the side for stirring in.

PREP AHEAD

The base for this soup can be made 1 week ahead, then strained and refrigerated or frozen. Don't add the noodles, shrimp and fresh herbs until just before serving.

THE SKINNY

No oil here, and the lime, ginger and spice–infused broth is a mouthwatering base for the noodles and shrimp.

Celeriac and roasted garlic soup with chives

preparation time 15 minutes / cooking time 50 minutes / serves 4

Celeriac, or celery root as it's sometimes called, is one of my favorite winter root vegetables. Its starchy nature makes it an ideal ingredient for soup or mash. Roasted garlic and celery salt inject a little more pizzazz for a very comforting thick soup.

1 bulb garlic
1½ tablespoons olive oil
1 large onion, chopped
2 celery ribs, finely diced
¼ teaspoon celery salt
½ large celeriac, peeled and chopped
   (about 9 ounces peeled)
4 cups vegetable broth
½ bunch chives, finely chopped
sea salt
black pepper

Preheat the oven to 375°F.
Cut the top third off the bulb of garlic and discard. Drizzle the garlic with ½ tablespoon of the olive oil. Season with sea salt and freshly ground black pepper, wrap in foil and roast for 40 minutes or until tender.

Meanwhile, heat the remaining olive oil in a large saucepan over medium-high heat. Add the onion, celery and celery salt, season with pepper and cook for 8 minutes or until the onion is translucent. Add the celeriac and broth, partially cover, reduce the heat to low and simmer for 40 minutes or until the celeriac is tender.

When the garlic is ready, squeeze the cloves into the soup. Puree everything in a food processor or blender until smooth. Season to taste, then pour into large bowls and sprinkle with the chives.

PREP AHEAD

The soup can be made up to 2 days ahead and refrigerated or frozen.

THE SKINNY

You won't need as much oil to cook the onions and vegetables if you turn down the heat a bit lower; they will sweat slowly but you get the same result. All the ingredients here are pure goodness with hardly any fat.

Chicken, rice and chunky vegetable soup with mini Parmesan croutons

preparation time 15 minutes / cooking time 30 minutes / serves 4

My mother, Louise, made a legendary chicken soup that my sisters and I have struggled to replicate. She would slowly poach a whole bird and when it was finished, shower it with decadent fried croutons rolled in Parmesan. I started this recipe with her masterpiece in mind but have changed things a bit. This lightning-quick method uses chicken breast and vegetables poached in a hot stock, which keeps everything juicy, and I've given the croutons a skinny makeover — they're baked in olive oil and Parmesan.

4 cups good-quality chicken or vegetable broth
2 boneless, skinless chicken breast halves
4 carrots, cut into ¾-inch chunks
1 small celery heart with leaves, sliced into ¾-inch pieces
1 yellow onion, cut into large dice
⅛ cup basmati rice
1¼ cups frozen or fresh shelled peas
2 tablespoons flat-leaf (Italian) parsley, finely chopped

Croutons
2 slices sourdough bread, cut into ½-inch cubes
1 teaspoon olive oil
1 tablespoon grated Parmesan
sea salt
black pepper

Preheat the oven to 400°F.

Bring the broth to a boil in a saucepan. Add the chicken and simmer gently for 4 minutes. Add the carrots, celery and onion, turn off the heat but leave the pan on the stove and cover with a lid. Leave to sit for 25 minutes.

Meanwhile, boil the rice in plenty of water until al dente. Drain and set aside.

To make the croutons, place the bread on a baking sheet and toss with the oil, Parmesan and some sea salt and freshly ground black pepper. Bake for 6 minutes or until golden and crisp. Remove and allow to cool.

Remove the chicken from the broth and shred with two forks. Add the meat back to the broth, along with the peas, rice and parsley. Turn the heat back on to high and heat for a few minutes to warm the peas through. Serve in bowls with the croutons scattered over.

PREP AHEAD

The soup can be made up to 3 days ahead and stored in the fridge. Store the croutons separately.

THE SKINNY

Since everything is freshly poached in the soup, no oil is needed. The croutons only have a tiny bit of cheese and oil and lend the soup a salty, nutty kick.

Chipotle black bean soup with lime-pickled onion

preparation time 10 minutes / cooking time 25 minutes / serves 4

It's good to be able to reach into your cupboard and pull out enough ingredients to make soup and this is one of those types of soups. Although in a perfect world I'd like to soak my own beans, I never have the time. Canned beans work just as well and soak up all the aromatic spices. Tart lime-marinated onions top off the soup for a great combination. If you own a mandolin, use it to slice the onions paper thin.

1 tablespoon olive oil
4 cloves garlic, finely chopped
2 red onions, thinly sliced
1 tablespoon ground cumin
1 tablespoon smoked paprika
1 tablespoon hot pepper sauce
1 can (15 ounces) black beans, drained and rinsed
3⅛ cups vegetable broth
juice of 2 limes
light sour cream, cilantro leaves and crisp tortillas, to serve

Lime-pickled onion
juice of 2 limes
1 small red onion, thinly sliced
sea salt
black pepper

To make the lime-pickled onion, combine the lime juice and onion in a small nonreactive bowl and season with sea salt and freshly ground black pepper. Leave to pickle for 30 minutes.

Meanwhile, heat the olive oil in a saucepan over medium–high heat. Add the garlic and onion and season. Saute for 8 minutes or until translucent. Add the spices and hot pepper sauce, cook for 1 minute, then add the beans, broth and lime juice. Simmer for 15 minutes, then puree. Pour everything back into a clean saucepan to reheat. Serve with a little of the drained pickled onion. Top with a small spoonful of sour cream and some cilantro and the tortillas on the side.

PREP AHEAD

This can be made 2 days ahead but don't make the onions until the day of serving. This soup freezes well.

THE SKINNY

Beans are immensely healthy and "stick to your ribs", keeping hunger pangs at bay. When paired with smoky chiles and lime, they transform into gorgeous soups and stews.

Vietnamese shrimp, rice, tomato and dill soup

preparation time 10 minutes / **cooking time** 15 minutes / **serves** 4

Some Vietnamese dishes are so simple it doesn't seem possible. Because of their purity, they don't require many ingredients or complicated cooking. This was one of my favorite soups I experienced while there. Dill seems like a strange herb to use in Asia, but because of the French occupation, copious amounts are used. This might sound like a lot of dill but it really works.

1⅛ cups basmati rice,
   not rinsed
5½ cups chicken broth
2 tablespoons fish sauce
2½-inch piece of fresh ginger,
   peeled and shredded
juice of 2 limes
6 large plum tomatoes,
   seeds removed and diced
¾ pound raw shrimp, peeled and
   deveined with tails left on
3 tablespoons chopped dill
1 small handful cilantro leaves, roughly
   chopped

Place the rice in a small saucepan, add enough water to cover by 2½ inches, cover with a lid and bring to a boil. Reduce the heat to medium-low and simmer for 8 minutes or until al dente. Drain and set aside.

Bring the broth to a boil in a large saucepan and add the cooked rice, fish sauce, ginger, lime juice, tomatoes, shrimp and dill. Simmer for a few minutes until the shrimp are cooked. Serve in bowls sprinkled with the cilantro scattered over.

PREP AHEAD

This is best prepared just before serving.

THE SKINNY

The rice and shrimp keep this light soup filling and there isn't a drop of oil in sight.

Gazpacho with apple salsa

preparation time 10 minutes / chilling time 3 hours / serves 6

When the weather is steamy hot there is no other food that refreshes you like gazpacho, and with the addition of crisp sour Granny Smith apple, even more so. I never tire of it and there are endless ways to play around with this soup, whether it's adding chile or using different colored tomatoes. Ripe and tasty vegetables are a must for this, so summer is the best time to make it.

2 ounces ripe juicy tomatoes
1 small cucumber, peeled
1 white or red onion
1 yellow or red bell pepper, seeds removed
2 tablespoons extra virgin olive oil, plus extra for drizzling
1 tablespoon sherry vinegar
1 teaspoon smoked paprika
2 thick slices white crusty bread, roughly torn
1¾ cups vegetable or chicken broth, chilled
1 Granny Smith apple
sea salt

Roughly chop all the vegetables, reserving a small amount of each before chopping. Place the chopped vegetables, olive oil, vinegar, paprika, bread and broth in a food processor and season with sea salt. Puree until very smooth.

Finely dice the reserved vegetables to make about 1 cup. Core and finely dice the apple. Mix with the chopped vegetables and set the salsa aside. At this point you can chill the soup for 3 hours or pour immediately over cups of ice to serve. Scatter over the salsa mixture and drizzle with a bit of olive oil to serve.

PREP AHEAD

This can be made 1 day ahead and refrigerated.

THE SKINNY

Food doesn't get healthier than this with blitzed raw veggies and broth. A little oil is used but it's quite minimal. Get your five-a-day with this icy treat.

Chilled crab, cucumber and yogurt soup

preparation time 10 minutes / chilling time 2 hours / serves 4

There is not a truer saying than "cool as a cucumber." Their watery nature is pure refreshment when the weather's hot. Combined with yogurt, hot pepper sauce and scallion, it makes a delicious chilly soup. Be sure to use cold broth because it can go sludgy if puréed with hot liquid. Make your stock and add some ice cubes to cool it quickly.

2 small cucumbers, peeled
1 small avocado, cut into chunks
2 teaspoons hot pepper sauce
6 scallions, thinly sliced
2 tablespoons chopped cilantro
1⅛ cups vegetable broth, chilled
juice of 2 limes
4 ounces low-fat plain yogurt
4 ounces crabmeat
sea salt
black pepper

Chop all but one-quarter of the cucumber into chunks. Place in a blender and add the avocado, 1½ teaspoons of the hot pepper sauce, half the scallions and cilantro, the broth, lime juice and yogurt and season with sea salt and freshly ground black pepper. Blend until very smooth. Pour into a container and refrigerate for 2 hours or until chilled.

Remove the seeds from the remaining cucumber and finely dice the flesh. Place in a small bowl, add the crabmeat and the remaining hot pepper sauce, scallions and cilantro and combine. Set aside.

Pour the soup into bowls and top with a dollop of crab mixture before serving. Crack plenty of black pepper over.

PREP AHEAD

The soup is best made on the day otherwise the avocado will turn a greyish color.

THE SKINNY

Unlike other soups, no oil is required to make this cold spicy soup any better.

Caramelized onion and fennel soup with cavolo nero and barley

preparation time 10 minutes / cooking time 30 minutes / serves 4

Caramelized onion soup is a winter treat. Here the traditional cheesy crouton has been replaced with greens and chewy barley to keep it full of goodness and flavor.

1 tablespoon olive oil
4 yellow onions, thinly sliced
3 fennel bulbs, cores removed
   and thinly sliced
3 cloves garlic, chopped
1 teaspoon finely chopped rosemary
   or thyme
1 large pinch of superfine sugar
¼ cup pearled barley or farro
4 cups vegetable broth
1 tablespoon brandy
3½ ounces Tuscan black kale (cavolo
   nero), stalks discarded and leaves
   thinly sliced
crusty bread, to serve

Heat the olive oil in a large saucepan over medium heat. Add the onions, fennel, garlic and rosemary and season well with sea salt, freshly ground black pepper and the sugar. Reduce the heat to low and cook for 20 minutes or until golden.

While the vegetables are cooking, bring a saucepan of salted water to a boil. Add the barley and cook for 10 minutes or until al dente, then drain.

When the vegetables are done, pour in the broth and brandy and bring to a boil. Add the kale and cook for 5 minutes, then add the barley. Taste for seasoning and serve in large bowls with some bread.

PREP AHEAD

The soup can be made 2 days ahead. It can be frozen but may need a little extra broth to thin it out on reheating because the barley absorbs some of it.

THE SKINNY

If you slowly saute onions over low heat, very little oil is needed. barley and farro are extremely good sources of fiber and they keep you full.

Chinese hot and sour mushroom soup

preparation time 15 minutes / soaking time 15 minutes / cooking time 10 minutes / serves 4

The Chinese consider hot foods, such as this, "yang", and cold foods "yin". The yang is reputed to increase your energy, so if you feel tired, have a comforting bowl of this to get your system moving and your yin/yang balance back on track. It's important to use white pepper because it provides the "hot" while the black vinegar delivers the signature sour taste.

8 dried shiitake mushrooms
1 tablespoon sesame oil
1¼-inch piece of fresh ginger,
    cut into 6 slices
4 ounces small button mushrooms, sliced
4 cups chicken or beef broth
2 ounces canned bamboo shoots,
    drained, rinsed and cut into julienne
2 tablespoons light soy sauce
3 tablespoons Chinese black vinegar
½ teaspoon freshly ground white pepper
4 ounces firm tofu, drained and cut into
    ½ inch pieces
1 egg, lightly beaten
1 tablespoon water
1 tablespoon cornstarch
sliced scallions, to serve

Soak the dried mushrooms in boiling water for 15 minutes, then drain and squeeze out the excess water. Remove the stems and finely chop the caps.

Heat the sesame oil in a large saucepan over medium-high heat. Add the ginger, all the mushrooms and saute for 3 minutes or until browned at the edges. Add the broth and bring to a boil. Add the bamboo shoots, soy, vinegar, pepper and tofu.

Slowly pour the beaten egg into the soup while stirring.

Mix the water with the cornstarch to make a paste. Pour into the soup and stir until it thickens. Serve in bowls with some scallion scattered over.

PREP AHEAD

This can be made 1 day ahead and refrigerated.

THE SKINNY

With the exception of the egg and sesame oil, this is ideal skinny food. With the tofu as protein, it's a very satisfying meal.

Pea and watercress soup

preparation time 15 minutes / cooking time 15 minutes / serves 4

Whiz up this neon green soup in any season and serve warm or chilled. When fresh peas aren't in season, frozen peas are a versatile stand-in for soups, salads or stews. Their quality is remarkable and they remain a much brighter green than fresh ones. Watercress lends a peppery kick.

1 teaspoon olive oil
1 yellow onion, chopped
1 small red-skinned potato,
   peeled and diced
1½ pounds frozen or fresh shelled peas
3½ cups vegetable or chicken broth
7 ounces picked watercress,
   roughly chopped
2 tablespoons chopped mint
soft bread, to serve
sea salt
black pepper

Heat the olive oil in a saucepan over medium–high heat. Add the onion and potato, season with sea salt and freshly ground black pepper and saute for 5 minutes or until softened. Add the peas and broth and bring to a simmer. Add the watercress and three-quarters of the mint and cook for another 10 minutes. Puree the mixture, in batches, in a food processor or blender. Pour back into the saucepan to reheat, or cover and refrigerate if serving chilled. Serve in big bowls with the remaining mint scattered over. Eat with a thick slice of soft bread to keep it substantial.

PREP AHEAD

The soup can be made 1 day ahead and refrigerated, and it freezes well too.

THE SKINNY

Peas are quite filling and a great freezer staple to make quick soups or purees.

Skinny *Meals in Heels*

Tomato, chickpea and cumin soup

preparation time 10 minutes / cooking time 30 minutes / serves 4

This is another easy soup to pull together from your pantry. Cumin when left whole has a more pronounced flavor than ground and, along with the sweet cinnamon, makes this peasant-style soup subtle and aromatic.

2 tablespoons olive oil
1 large yellow onion, chopped
1 large carrot, diced
2 clove garlics, chopped
1½-inch piece of fresh ginger, finely chopped
1 teaspoon cumin seeds
1 teaspoon hot smoked paprika
2 cinnamon sticks
2 cups vegetable or chicken broth
1 can (14 ounces) whole plum tomatoes
1 can (15 ounces) chickpeas, drained and rinsed
finely grated zest and juice of 1 lemon
sea salt
black pepper

Heat the olive oil in a large saucepan over medium-high heat. Add the onion, carrot, garlic and ginger, season with sea salt and freshly ground black pepper and saute for 8 minutes or until the vegetables have softened and are golden. Add the spices and cook for another minute. Pour in the broth, tomatoes and add a little more salt. Break up the tomatoes with a flat spoon. Cook for 15 minutes or until all the flavors come together. Add the chickpeas and lemon zest and juice and cook for another 5 minutes to warm through.

PREP AHEAD

The entire soup can be made 2 days ahead and refrigerated. It also freezes successfully.

THE SKINNY

Chickpeas are high in fiber, which, in addition to the ginger, onion and garlic, is supposed to keep your digestive system clean and healthy.

Weekday Dinners
In Under One Hour

Spicy lamb kebabs with pomegranate seeds, herb salad and chile sauce

preparation time 10 minutes / **cooking time** 5 minutes / **serves** 4

The sauce here sounds odd but, trust me, it really works. When dried red chile or harissa is mixed with vinegar, it creates a wondrous sauce that isn't too spicy. The vinegar cuts the heat and balances out the flavors. The lamb skewers are marinated with it, then broiled and wrapped up with ruby pomegranate seeds, fresh herbs and Greek-style yogurt for a mouthwatering kebab.

1 pound 2 ounces leg of lamb, trimmed of all fat
3 tablespoons harissa
2 tablespoons red wine vinegar
1 pomegranate
1 handful mint leaves
1 handful flat-leaf (Italian) parsley leaves
1 small red onion, thinly sliced into half moons
Greek-style yogurt, lavash bread and lettuce, to serve
sea salt
black pepper

Preheat a broiler to very high. Cut the lamb into 1¼-inch chunks and season well with sea salt and freshly ground black pepper. Mix the harissa with the vinegar. Thread the lamb onto metal or soaked wooden skewers. Brush some of the harissa mixture on both sides of the lamb. Broil for 2 minutes each side.

Halve the pomegranate and pound the halves with a wooden spoon over a large bowl. Remove any white membrane from the seeds.

Serve the lamb with the herbs, pomegranate seeds, a dollop of the remaining harissa mixture, onion, yogurt and crisp lettuce all wrapped up in the flat bread.

PREP AHEAD

The lamb can be marinated and refrigerated 1 day ahead.

THE SKINNY

Pastes such as harissa are an instant and skinny way to add flavor to meat or veg. My favorite are the dark chunky mixes made with good-quality dried chiles.

Greek pork burgers with tomato salad and radish tzatziki

preparation time 15 minutes / cooking time 10 minutes / serves 4

Fresh oregano is such a pungent herb and these grilled pork burgers come alive with its woodsy taste. Garlicky tzatziki gains an edge with crisp chopped radishes swirled through. Serve with a fresh tomato salad or rice for the perfect summer or winter meal.

1 pound 2 ounces very lean ground pork
2 handfuls soft fresh bread crumbs
1 small red onion, finely chopped
½ clove garlic, crushed or finely
   chopped
finely grated zest of 1 lemon
2 tablespoons oregano leaves,
   finely chopped
1 egg
cooking oil or spray
sea salt
black pepper

Radish tzatziki
¾ cup low-fat Greek-style yogurt
1 tablespoon chopped dill
16 small radishes, roughly chopped
   or sliced
½ clove garlic, crushed
   or finely chopped
juice of ½ lemon

Mix together the pork, bread crumbs, onion, garlic, lemon zest, oregano and egg and season with a good amount of sea salt and freshly ground black pepper. Mix well and form into 12 flat burgers. Refrigerate until using.

To make the radish tzatziki, mix all the ingredients together and season.

Heat a grill or grill pan to high. Rub the burgers with a tiny bit of oil or spray and cook for 2–3 minutes each side. Serve with the tzatziki alongside.

PREP AHEAD

The burgers can be made 1 day ahead and refrigerated. They freeze well, too — just thaw in the fridge on the day of using.

THE SKINNY

If you use extra-lean pork, these aren't too caloric. The fresh bread crumbs soften them up so you don't need extra fat. Oil spray keeps the fat content down when cooking too.

Lamb tenderloins with Parmesan pea puree

preparation time 15 minutes / cooking time 10 minutes / serves 4

Peas, mint and lamb are a dream trio. The flavors all dovetail together in perfect unison for a quick and simple midweek meal. Edamame could also be used for an even healthier puree.

2 tablespoons balsamic vinegar
1 teaspoon extra virgin olive oil
2 cloves garlic, finely chopped
1 tablespoon whole-grain mustard
1 tablespoon honey
1 small handful mint leaves, chopped
4 lean lamb tenderloins (about 1 pound 2 ounces), trimmed of all fat
sea salt
black pepper

Parmesan pea puree
3⅔ cups shelled frozen or fresh peas
1 small handful mint leaves, chopped
4 scallions, chopped
½ cup vegetable or chicken broth
2 tablespoons shredded Parmesan

Mix the vinegar, olive oil, garlic, mustard, honey and mint together and season with sea salt and freshly ground black pepper. Coat the lamb tenderloins with the marinade and set aside.

To make the Parmesan pea puree, blanch the peas in salted boiling water for 1–2 minutes. Drain, then puree in a food processor with the mint, scallions, broth, Parmesan and some salt. Pour into a saucepan to reheat.

Heat a grill, broiler or grill pan to high. Cook the lamb tenderloins for about 2 minutes each side for medium. Allow to rest for 3 minutes, covered with foil, then serve with the pea puree.

PREP AHEAD

The lamb can be marinated 1 day ahead and refrigerated. Make the pea puree on the night of serving, otherwise the color will gray a bit.

THE SKINNY

Avoid lamb chops, which have a lot more fat. Tenderloins are usually trimmed very lean but still have all the taste and tenderness of the other cuts.

Pork and fennel roast with lemon and cilantro paste

preparation time 10 minutes / **cooking time** 30 minutes / **serves** 4

Spice pastes are a clever way to bump up a pan of roasted vegetables and meat. Preserved lemon, smoked paprika and cilantro are pureed together to make a sticky, citrus paste that is very special indeed.

2 large red-skinned potatoes, scrubbed, cut into 1-inch pieces
2 fennel bulbs, quartered and cores removed
3 red onions, quartered
2 pork tenderloins (about ¾ pound each), halved lengthwise and then crosswise so you have 8 pieces
Greek-style yogurt, to serve
sea salt
black pepper

Lemon and cilantro paste

4 large preserved lemon quarters
1 clove garlic
½ thumb-sized red chile, seeds removed
1 teaspoon smoked paprika
1 tablespoon honey
1 tablespoon chopped cilantro
1 tablespoon olive oil
1 tablespoon water

Preheat the oven to 400°F. Drop the potato and fennel into a saucepan of lightly salted boiling water. Return to a boil, then cook for 1 minute. Drain well and spread out onto a tea towel–lined tray to dry.

To make the lemon and cilantro paste, rinse the preserved lemon under running water. Discard the pulp and transfer the rinds to a food processor. Add the remaining ingredients and process into a smooth puree.

Place all the vegetables and pork in a large roasting pan or two small ones. Rub the paste over the pork and a little bit on the veg as well. Season with sea salt and freshly ground black pepper and bake for 25 minutes or until the pork is cooked and the vegetables are golden. Serve with the yogurt.

PREP AHEAD

The paste can be made 1 week ahead and refrigerated in an airtight container, drizzled with a little oil to keep it fresh.

THE SKINNY

Pastes such as this are wonderful because they create a sweet–sour glaze. Pork tenderloin is the leanest cut you can get, meltingly tender and fairly inexpensive.

Gaucho skirt steak with avocado and hearts of palm salad

preparation time 10 minutes / cooking time 10 minutes / serves 4

Dried Mexican chiles make incredible smoky rubs for meat. Toast them in a skillet, then whiz them up in a spice grinder. It's worth this small amount of effort because home-ground chiles are so much fresher than store-bought ground mixes. Each variety of chile has its own unique taste; ancho is very fruity while pasilla has a chocolate scent. If you don't have access to whole Mexican dried chiles, then use a good-quality ground chiles.

2 dried ancho or pasilla chiles
(or 2 tablespoons pasilla or
ancho chile powder)
1 tablespoon smoked sweet paprika
1 teaspoon unsweetened cocoa powder
1 pound 5 ounces skirt steak or
4 lean sirloin steaks
1 teaspoon olive oil
1 tablespoon superfine sugar

Salad

1 can (14 ounces) hearts of palm,
drained and sliced
1 large avocado, cut into chunky pieces
juice of 1 lime
10 cherry tomatoes, halved
1 small handful cilantro, chopped
1 teaspoon olive oil

Heat a nonstick skillet over high heat until very hot. Toast the chiles for 30 seconds each side or until they puff up. Remove the stems and seeds. Roughly chop and place in a spice grinder with the smoked paprika and cocoa powder and process until ground. (The paprika will keep it dry and make it less sticky in the spice grinder.)

Rub the meat on both sides with the olive oil. Mix the sugar, about 1 teaspoon of sea salt and the ground chile mixture together and sprinkle on both sides of the steaks.

To make the salad, mix all the ingredients together and season.

Heat a grill, broiler or grill pan to high. Cook the steaks for 3 minutes each side for medium-rare.

Rest for 5 minutes, covered. Slice and serve with the salad.

PREP AHEAD

The rub can be made a week ahead and stored in a screw-top jar to keep fresh. Make the salad just before eating to keep the colors vibrant.

THE SKINNY

A little bit of avocado is fine and goes well with red meat. Chile rubs boost any type of broiled meat for almost no calories but enormous taste.

Sizzling Korean-style beef with sesame seeds

preparation time 15 minutes / cooking time 5 minutes / serves 4

Bulgogi, with its paper-thin slices of beef seared quickly with garlic and soy, is one of the best-known Korean dishes. The trick to making the beef ultra thin is to partially freeze it and then slice it. Sirloin steak when cut this way is very tender and, best of all, affordable.

1 pound 2 ounces beef sirloin
   or round steak, trimmed
3 tablespoons superfine sugar
3 tablespoons soy sauce
2 tablespoons mirin
2 cloves garlic, finely chopped
1 thumb-sized red chile, seeds removed
   and sliced
1 teaspoon sesame oil
vegetable oil, for cooking
8 scallions, cut into 1¼-inch pieces
1 tablespoon sesame seeds, toasted
steamed rice, to serve

Thinly slice the beef. If you have any extra time, it helps if the meat is partially frozen, allowing you to slice it even thinner. Ten minutes in the freezer will help immensely. Combine the sugar, soy, mirin, garlic, chile and sesame oil in a bowl. Add the beef and stir well to coat. Crack some black pepper over as well.

Heat a scant amount of vegetable oil in a wok over high heat until very hot. Cook half of the beef for 40 seconds, turning until browned, then remove from the wok and repeat with a little more oil and the remaining beef. Return all of the beef to the wok and add the scallions. Stir-fry for 1 minute, then add the sesame seeds. Serve with the rice.

PREP AHEAD

Marinate the meat the night before and refrigerate it (or freeze it and simply thaw in the refrigerator on the day of cooking).

THE SKINNY

Soy and mirin are optimal skinny ingredients for stir-fries as they aren't caloric and add savory taste.

Lamb with borlotti beans, basil oil and roasted cherry tomatoes

preparation time 10 minutes / cooking time 20 minutes / serves 4

My family and I put this combination together when we stayed near Nice, in France, one summer. Baskets of fresh pink-spotted borlotti beans were overflowing in the market and I was desperate to use them. They don't appear often so you have to act on it when you see them. At home I use canned, which are still very good.

12 ounces cherry tomatoes
   on the vine
2 cloves garlic, finely chopped
3 tablespoons extra virgin olive oil
1 large handful basil leaves, chopped
4 tablespoons balsamic vinegar
1 can (15 ounces) borlotti beans,
   drained and rinsed
1 pound 2 ounce lamb tenderloins,
   trimmed
sea salt
black pepper

Preheat the oven to 350°F. Place the tomatoes on a baking sheet with half of the garlic and drizzle with 1 tablespoon of the olive oil. Roast for 15 minutes or until slightly collapsed.

Mix the basil and vinegar and remaining garlic and olive oil together and season with sea salt and freshly ground black pepper. Place the beans in a large skillet and pour over three-quarters of the basil mixture. Gently cook over low heat until warmed through.

Preheat the broiler or a grill pan to high. Rub the remaining basil mixture over the lamb and season. Cook for 2 minutes each side for medium-rare and serve with the beans and tomatoes.

PREP AHEAD

The basil mixture can be made a couple of hours ahead and the lamb marinated as well. Just before serving, prepare the tomatoes and warm beans and cook the lamb.

THE SKINNY

The sweet balsamic vinegar makes up for the need for excess oil in the herb dressing. Beans are satisfying, healthy and a quick base for salads or grilled meats.

Steak with balsamic mushroom sauce and shoestring root vegetables

preparation time 20 minutes / cooking time 40 minutes / serves 4

Steak and mushrooms is a classic. Add a reduction of balsamic vinegar to the sauce to make it even more lip-smacking. Scoop up the sauce with roasted root vegetables and serve a fresh green salad on the side. Try to use a balsamic that is midrange in price, not the cheapest or the dearest but fairly good quality.

1½ pound mixed root vegetables (such as celeriac, carrot and parsnips), peeled
olive oil spray
finely grated zest of 1 lemon
2 tablespoons olive oil
18 ounces button mushrooms, trimmed and sliced
2 cloves garlic, finely chopped
¼ cup balsamic vinegar
2 tablespoons light brown sugar
4 beef steaks, tenderloin or sirloin (4 to 5 ounces each), trimmed of all fat
2 tablespoons finely chopped flat-leaf (Italian) parsley
sea salt
black pepper

Preheat the oven to 375°F. Slice the vegetables into matchsticks, about 1⁄16 inch thick (a mandoline or food processor attachment is very handy for this). Place on 2 baking sheets and spray with olive oil. Sprinkle with the lemon zest and season with sea salt and freshly ground black pepper. Roast for 40 minutes or until crisp.

Heat the olive oil in a large skillet over high heat. Add the mushrooms and garlic along with a good pinch of salt. Cook for 5 minutes or until the mushrooms are browned. Mix the vinegar and sugar together and pour over the mushrooms. Stir to combine and cook for 1–2 minutes or until the mixture becomes syrupy. Set aside.

Heat a grill, broiler or grill pan to high. Season the steaks and cook for 2–3 minutes each side, depending on the thickness of the steaks, for medium-rare. Rest for 5 minutes, then reheat the mushroom sauce, adding any resting juices from the meat. Serve with the crisp vegetables and a sprinkle of parsley over everything.

PREP AHEAD

The mushroom sauce can be made a couple of hours before and then reheated. The vegetables can be sliced 4 hours ahead and kept in cold water. Drain well on a kitchen towel before baking.

THE SKINNY

Steak is assumed to be fattening but it doesn't have to be. Buy lean cuts and trim off excess fat. Balsamic vinegar is a faultless skinny ingredient in sauces that normally use butter or cream.

Beef and pea keema curry

preparation time 10 minutes / cooking time 30 minutes / serves 4

My Indian friend Rita gave me this recipe. Her family calles it "hamburger curry" because it uses ground beef. Keema translates as "ground" and it's considered the nursery food of India. Children, though, aren't the only ones to find it comforting and tasty. It's pretty mild in heat and spice, so if you want it hotter, just throw in some chile flakes. I like to use standard curry powder that's typically bright yellow in color. Be sure to use a fresh fragrant one. Spices lose their punch after six to eight months so check your spice cabinet first.

2 teaspoons vegetable oil
1 pound 2 ounces lean ground beef
1 large onion, finely chopped
2 cloves garlic, chopped
1 tablespoon finely chopped fresh ginger
1 large baking potato, cut into 1¼-inch cubes
2 carrots, cut into 1¼-inch chunks
2 tablespoons mild curry powder
1 tablespoon tomato paste
2 cups beef or vegetable broth
½ cup frozen or fresh shelled peas
steamed basmati rice, cilantro leaves and mango or lime chutney, to serve
sea salt
black pepper

Heat 1 teaspoon of the vegetable oil in a nonstick skillet over high heat. Add the beef and cook for about 5 minutes or until crisp and browned, breaking up any clumps with the back of a wooden spoon. Remove from the pan, discarding the fat, and set aside.

Wipe out the pan and heat the remaining oil. Add the onion, garlic and fresh ginger and season with sea salt and freshly ground black pepper. Cook for 8 minutes or until softened. Add the potato, carrots and curry powder and cook for another couple of minutes. Add the tomato paste, broth and ground beef and stir together. Reduce the heat to medium and cook for 15 minutes. During the last 5 minutes, add the peas. Serve with the basmati rice, cilantro leaves and mango or lime chutney.

PREP AHEAD

The curry can be made 1–2 days ahead and refrigerated or frozen. Gently reheat, adding a little extra broth or water as it will have thickened up.

THE SKINNY

Usually ground meat is fattening but if you buy lean ground steak, it can still be healthy. With three types of vegetables included, this is a one-pot healthy meal.

Mirin and soy-poached beef and onion stew

preparation time 15 minutes / cooking time 10 minutes / serves 4

⬦⬦⬦⬦⬦⬦⬦⬦⬦⬦⬦⬦⬦⬦⬦⬦⬦⬦⬦⬦⬦⬦⬦⬦⬦⬦⬦⬦⬦⬦

This unusually prepared Japanese dish is called *oyakodon*. The beef is quickly poached in a tasty mirin and soy broth and served over rice. Traditionally a beaten egg is poured into the poaching liquid to thicken it. I have left this out to keep it slimmer but it's an option you can choose.

1 pound 2 ounce top round steak
1⅛ cup vegetable broth
7 tablespoons soy sauce
¾ cup plus 2 tablespoons mirin
2 tablespoons superfine sugar
2 yellow onions, thinly sliced into half moons
1 tablespoon chopped pickled ginger
6 scallions, finely chopped
1 thumb-sized red chile, seeds removed and thinly sliced
steamed rice, to serve

Place the beef in the freezer while you prepare the other ingredients. Combine the broth, soy, mirin and sugar in a saucepan, bring to a boil, then reduce the heat to a simmer. Add the onions and cook for 5 minutes.

Thinly slice the beef, add to the saucepan, then remove from the heat. Divide the soup among bowls and sprinkle with the pickled ginger, scallions and chile. Serve with the rice.

••

PREP AHEAD

The meat can be sliced and poaching liquid prepared up to 8 hours ahead.

THE SKINNY

Poaching is a slim method to cook meat, keeping it juicy without using fat. The soy and mirin provide a delicious sauce, so you won't feel like you're missing out on anything.

Skinny *Meals in Heels*

Pork scaloppine with lemon-wine sauce

preparation time 20 minutes / cooking time 25 minutes / serves 4

Traditionally this would be done with veal, which is both expensive and not very politically correct to eat, but pork tenderloin makes a shoo-in substitute and is equally tender.

14-ounce pork tenderloin
all-purpose flour, for dusting
1 tablespoon olive oil
3 small French shallots (eschalots),
   finely chopped
juice of 1 lemon
1 cup chicken broth
1 cup white wine
1 tablespoon baby capers in brine,
   drained
2 tablespoons finely chopped flat-leaf
   (Italian) parsley
cooked Puy (French) lentils, smashed
   boiled baby potatoes
   or blanched broccoli, to serve
sea salt
black pepper

Slice the pork crosswise into ½-inch-thick pieces, then gently pound between sheets of parchment paper using a rolling pin or meat pounder until about ⅛ inch thick. Season well with sea salt and freshly ground black pepper and dust with flour.

Heat a large nonstick skillet over high heat until very hot. Heat 1 teaspoon of the olive oil, add one-quarter of the pork scallops and cook for 1–2 minutes each side or until browned. Remove from the skillet and repeat with the remaining pork and olive oil. It's important to keep the skillet really hot or the pork will stick and need more oil. Remove from the skillet.

Add the shallots to the skillet, season and cook until soft. Add the lemon juice, broth and wine and cook for 5 minutes or until reduced by half. Return the meat to the skillet along with the capers and cook for 30 seconds or until just heated through. Scatter with chopped parsley and serve with lentils, potatoes or broccoli if you like.

PREP AHEAD

The pork can be sliced and pounded 1 day ahead and refrigerated, stored between sheets of parchment paper.

THE SKINNY

Lemon, capers and wine create a tasty sauce without the need for cream or butter.
Pork tenderloin cooks quickly and is very low in fat.

No-cream Swedish meatballs with dill

preparation time 15 minutes / cooking time 20 minutes / serves 4

Everyone adores meatballs. They're the perfect comfort food. They're just fun to eat, plain and simple. Swedish food is one of my favorite cuisines but with the cream added to most dishes, it's a bit fattening. Reduced beef broth and dill create a tasty sauce here.

1 pound 2 ounces lean ground pork
2 teaspoons ground allspice
1 egg
1 small onion, finely diced
⅓ cup fresh white bread crumbs
1 tablespoon olive oil
1 tablespoon all-purpose flour
½ cup white wine
1¾ cups beef broth
1 tablespoon finely chopped dill
canned cranberry sauce, to serve
boiled green vegetables or potatoes,
    to serve (optional)
sea salt
black pepper

Preheat the oven to 375°F. Combine the pork with the allspice, egg, onion and bread crumbs in a bowl and season with sea salt and freshly ground black pepper. Mix well and form into golf ball–sized meatballs. Place on a large baking sheet, toss with a bit of the olive oil and season. Bake for 15 minutes or until browned. You won't need to turn them. When you remove them, use a metal spatula to scrape them from the baking sheet.

Heat the remaining olive oil in a nonstick skillet over medium-low heat. Add the flour and cook for 2 minutes or until lightly browned, then add the wine and broth. Whisk until it is a thick sauce. Add the meatballs to the skillet and cook for 2–3 minutes or until well coated. Sprinkle with the dill and serve with the cranberry sauce and vegetables or potatoes.

PREP AHEAD

The meatballs can be rolled 1 day ahead and refrigerated or frozen. They can be baked and frozen as well.

THE SKINNY

Baking meatballs requires far less oil than pan-frying. The fresh dill lifts the sauce and compensates for the lack of cream.

Stir-frying: the definitive guide

This genius method of cooking is quick, healthy and makes the perfect one-pot meal with rice or noodles. Mix and match your ingredients for a delicious lunch or dinner.

EQUIPMENT You will need a large wok and two long wooden spoons to cook with. Asian supermarkets are the best places to buy them and they are inexpensive. The best type of wok is carbon steel.

To season a new wok, place it over high heat until nearly smoking. Dip some kitchen paper in vegetable oil and wipe the surface of the wok — use tongs as it will be very hot. Place the wok back over low heat and heat for 10 minutes. Remove and allow to cool. Rinse with water (never soap) and wipe the surface with a bit more oil. It's now ready to use.

Whenver you are stir-frying, always heat the wok until smoking hot, then add your oil. After using, always wipe with oil to prevent rust from forming.

COMBINATIONS Try to choose one protein and one to three vegetables. One of the vegetables should be crisp, like pepper or broccoli, so there is a contrast in textures. Too many ingredients isn't good either — less is more!

PREPARATION Before you start to cook, it's important to have everything ready to go. The cooking time is short so chop all the ingredients, make the sauce and cook the rice before stir-frying.

THE ESSENTIAL FLAVOR BASE This is the base for any of the suggested sauces. It is wok-fried just before the vegetables are added:

- 1 thumb-sized red chile, seeds removed and sliced
- 2 cloves garlic, sliced
- 1½-inch piece of fresh ginger, shredded

COMPONENTS It's as easy as choosing your protein, two to four types of vegetables and then your sauce.

Protein To serve four people, 1 pound 2 ounces of meat or seafood is a good guide. If using tofu, then reduce the quantity to 14 ounces. If you like, to add more flavor and give a crisp edge to your protein, mix your meat, seafood or tofu with 1 teaspoon of soy sauce and 1 tablespoon of cornstarch. The following proteins are ideal for stir-frying.

- turkey breast cutlets, cut into ¼-inch-thick slices
- chicken (thigh or breast) boneless, skinless, cut into 1¼-inch-thick slices
- beef or pork, cut into 1¼ inch thick slices, or use lean ground meat
- sliced squid
- whole peeled raw shrimp
- 14 ounces drained and pressed firm tofu, cut into 1¼-inch cubes

Vegetables, crunch and noodles As with protein, 1 pound 2 ounces of vegetables or a mixture of noodles and veg is a good amount to feed four people. Choose one to four components for a well-balanced mix. For the vegetables, slice each into 1¼-inch pieces so they cook at the same time. These are some of my favorite vegetable and noodle additions to stir-fries.

- red or white onions or scallions
- red or yellow bell peppers
- broccoli
- green or yard-long beans
- Chinese vegetables like Chinese broccoli (gai larn), choy sum or bok choy
- cherry tomatoes
- chunks of pineapple
- bean sprouts

- savoy or napa cabbage
- kale
- carrot
- celery
- sugar snap peas or snow peas
- baby corn
- toasted cashews or roasted peanuts
- shiitake mushrooms or quartered button mushrooms
- water chestnuts or bamboo shoots
- noodles: soaked rice noodles, ramen, udon, somen, buckwheat,
  Chinese egg or fresh egg noodles

<u>Sauces</u> Use these sauce mixtures in addition to the essential flavor base (see opposite) with your choice of protein, vegetables and/or noodles. Each sauce makes a generous ¾ cup, so that you have a little extra to dribble on rice. Dark soy is preferable to regular soy sauce. It's aged with molasses and thickened with cornstarch, which results in a more full-bodied liquid that has much less salt.

Oyster or hoisin sauce (and black bean sauce)

Red meats like pork combined with greens, such as Chinese broccoli (gai larn), baby corn, red onion and water chestnuts are lovely with this.

2 tablespoons chicken broth
  or Shaoxing rice wine
2 tablespoons oyster or hoisin sauce
1 tablespoon light brown sugar

1 tablespoon lime juice
2 teaspoons dark or regular soy sauce
1 teaspoon cornstarch
  dissolved in 2 teaspoons water

Mix all the ingredients in a small bowl.

NOTE For a black bean sauce version, add 1 tablespoon salted black beans and 1 chopped clove garlic to the mixture.

Spicy Chinese Sichuan sauce

Chicken breast, broccoli, red onion and toasted cashews pair nicely with this sauce.

2 tablespoons chicken broth
2 tablespoons dark or regular soy sauce
1 tablespoon Chinese black vinegar
1 tablespoon Shaoxing rice wine

2 teaspoons chile bean sauce
2 teaspoons cornstarch
   dissolved in 1 tablespoon water
1 teaspoon superfine sugar

Mix all the ingredients in a small bowl and stir until the sugar has dissolved.

NOTE If you can't find Chinese black vinegar, use normal red wine vinegar. For a rice wine substitute, use dry sherry, and you can use any type of chile sauce or paste if you can't find the chile bean sauce.

Sweet and sour chili sauce

Especially notable with beef, green beans, julienned carrots and rice noodles.

2 tablespoons dark or regular soy sauce
2 tablespoons lime juice

4½ tablespoons Thai sweet chile sauce
2 teaspoons fish sauce

Mix all the ingredients in a small bowl.

Chinese lemon sauce

My best-loved combination with chicken breast, scallions and broccoli.

3 tablespoons chicken broth
3 tablespoons honey
1 tablespoon soy sauce

2 teaspoons cornstarch dissolved in 1 tablespoon
   water
½ teaspoon Chinese five-spice-powder
finely grated zest and juice of 2 lemons

Mix all the ingredients in a small bowl.

Southeast Asian lime and basil sauce

Chicken thighs, green beans, cherry tomatoes, fresh pineapple and red onion are my favorite combination to use with this sweet and sour sauce.

juice of 2 limes
3 tablespoons chicken broth
1 tablespoon fish sauce

1 tablespoon light brown sugar
1 tablespoon very finely chopped lemongrass
1 large handful Thai or regular basil leaves

Mix the lime juice, broth, fish sauce, sugar and lemongrass in a bowl. Add the basil leaves to the stir-fry at the very end of the cooking time.

NOTE This makes less liquid than the other sauces but this type of Thai/Vietnamese stir-fry doesn't use as much.

• •

Japanese soy, mirin and honey sauce

Foolproof with beef, shiitake mushrooms, scallions and noodles.

3 tablespoons mirin
2 tablespoons lime juice
2 tablespoons Japanese soy sauce

1 tablespoon honey
2 teaspoons cornstarch dissolved in 1 tablespoon
 water

Mix all the ingredients in a small bowl.

• •

Tamarind-glazed chicken with green chile, mint and tomato salad

preparation time 15 minutes / cooking time 10 minutes / serves 4

A sweet and sour tamarind glaze turns these chicken skewers into something special. Although you can just grill the chicken breasts with the sauce, it's much nicer on a skewer because you get more of the sticky sauce.

½ cup jarred tamarind puree
1 tablespoon finely grated fresh ginger
2 teaspoons mild ground chile pepper
2 teaspoons black or yellow mustard seeds
2 tablespoons honey
4 boneless, skinless chicken breast halves, cut into chunky 1¼-inch pieces
cooked basmati rice and low-fat Greek-style yogurt, to serve
sea salt
black pepper

Salad
9 ounces cherry tomatoes, halved
1 small red onion, sliced into half moons
1 small handful mint leaves, chopped
2 tablespoons chopped cilantro
1 thumb-sized green chile, seeds removed and thinly sliced
pinch of mild ground chile pepper
pinch of black or yellow mustard seeds
juice of ⅛ lemon

Combine the tamarind, ginger, ground chile pepper, mustard seeds and honey in a small bowl and season with sea salt and freshly ground black pepper. Soak some wooden skewers or use metal ones. Thread the chicken onto the skewers, brush with some of the marinade and set aside until cooking (see Note).

To make the salad, mix all the ingredients together and season.

Preheat a grill or broiler to high. Cook the chicken skewers for 2 minutes each side. Remove, brush heavily with the glaze and cook for another minute or until cooked through.

Serve with the salad, rice, remaining marinade and yogurt.

NOTE Be sure you set some marinade aside for serving to avoid cross-contamination with the raw chicken from the brush.

PREP AHEAD

The chicken can be marinated and threaded onto skewers 8 hours ahead. You can also freeze it this way and thaw it in the refrigerator on the day of cooking.

THE SKINNY

Tamarind puree is a zero calorie/fat ingredient that adds bags of flavor and doubles as a glaze.

Turkish chicken escalopes with yogurt marinade

preparation time 15 minutes / cooking time 10 minutes / serves 4

Yogurt not only tenderizes meat, it also makes an exceptional marinade. Flattening the chicken breasts may seem like an extra step but it makes them fork tender and decreases the cooking time. This is also very good with Turkish salsa (see page 20).

4 boneless, skinless chicken breasts
   halves
juice of 1 lemon
1 clove garlic, crushed through a press
¾ cup low-fat Greek-style yogurt
1 small onion, grated
1 teaspoon ground cumin
1 teaspoon ground coriander
1 teaspoon hot paprika
2 tablespoons chopped mint,
   plus extra leaves to serve
1 teaspoon olive oil
steamed basmati rice or a green salad,
   to serve
sea salt
black pepper

Halve each chicken breast horizontally so that you have two flat pieces. Place each piece between sheets of parchment paper and pound to about ⅝ inch with a rolling pin or meat mallet. Place in a glass dish or bowl and season well with sea salt and freshly ground black pepper. Add the lemon juice, garlic, yogurt, onion, spices and mint into the bowl.
Mix well and refrigerate until using.
   Preheat a grill or broiler to high. Drizzle the chicken with olive oil to keep it from sticking. Cook for about 3 minutes each side or until just cooked through.
   Sprinkle the chicken with the extra mint leaves. Serve with rice or a crisp green salad.

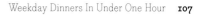

PREP AHEAD

The chicken can be marinated 1 day ahead and even frozen in the marinade.

THE SKINNY

Yogurt is a tremendous skinny ingredient for so many reasons. It can work as a marinade, dressing, instant sauce or it can be dolloped on a dish to finish instead of cream. Any spices, fresh herbs or jarred curry pastes are wonderful mixed with it as well.

Stuffed chicken breasts with spinach, cinnamon and dates

preparation time 10 minutes / cooking time 35 minutes / serves 4

This one-dish chicken dinner is stuffed with sweet caramelized onion, spinach and sticky dates and baked with sour pomegranate molasses. It's a wholesome combination and full of tantalizing tastes of the Middle East.

2 large onions, thinly sliced

2 cloves garlic, sliced

1 tablespoon olive oil

2 teaspoons ground cumin

4 large soft dates, pitted and chopped

7 ounces baby spinach

4 boneless, skinless chicken breast halves

1 teaspoon ground cinnamon

3 tablespoons pomegranate molasses or honey

steamed couscous or bulgur tossed with lemon juice and chopped parsley, to serve

sea salt

black pepper

Preheat the oven to 400°F.

In a large nonstick skillet over medium heat, saute the onions and garlic with a splash of olive oil and some sea salt and freshly ground black pepper for 10 minutes or until golden. Add the cumin, dates, spinach and a bit more seasoning and cook for another minute or two or until the spinach has wilted. Remove from the heat and cool.

Slice the chicken breasts horizontally without cutting all the way through so they open up like a book. Divide the stuffing among the breasts, fold the breasts back over and place in a shallow baking dish. Rub the cinnamon over the breasts and season. Drizzle with the pomegranate molasses and bake for 20 minutes or until just cooked through. Serve with the couscous.

PREP AHEAD

The breasts can be stuffed 1 day ahead and baked just before serving. They can also be frozen and thawed in the fridge on the day of using.

THE SKINNY

Dates are an excellent skinny ingredient, lending sweetness to savory food.

Tostadas with spicy tomato turkey

preparation time 10 minutes / cooking time 20 minutes / serves 4

───────◇◇◇◇◇◇───────

Ground turkey is a star ingredient as it's inexpensive, has practically nil fat and cooks up a pearly white color. Here it's pan fried with a spicy, tangy tomato sauce and served up on a crisp baked corn tortilla. You can also use flour wraps.

8 fresh corn tortillas
1 teaspoon olive oil, plus extra
   for brushing
1 onion, finely chopped
2 cloves garlic, chopped
1 pound 2 ounces ground turkey
1 tablespoon ground cumin
1 tablespoon smoked paprika
2 tablespoons light brown sugar
4¼ table spoons apple cider vinegar
1⅛ cups canned tomato puree or
   chopped tomatoes
1 avocado, chopped into chunks
1 small red onion, finely chopped
1 large handful cilantro, chopped
sea salt
black pepper

Preheat the oven to 400°F. Brush the tortillas on both sides with olive oil. Place in a single layer on a baking sheet and bake for 7–8 minutes or until crisp and golden. Remove and set aside.

Meanwhile, heat the olive oil in a large skillet over medium-high heat. Sauté the onion and garlic with some sea salt and freshly ground black pepper for about 5 minutes or until the onion has softened. Add the turkey and cook, breaking up the meat with the back of a spoon, for about 4 minutes or until thoroughly browned. Add the cumin, paprika, sugar, vinegar and tomato puree and cook for another 10 minutes or until most of the liquid has evaporated.

Spoon the meat over the tortillas and top with the avocado, onion and cilantro.

• •

PREP AHEAD

The turkey mixture can be made 1–2 days ahead and refrigerated. It can also be frozen and thawed in the fridge on the day of using.

THE SKINNY

Although you can use soft corn tortillas, it's just not the same as crunching into a crisp one. Brushing and baking is a clever way to replace deep-frying. Ground turkey is very lean but can cook up dry, so the tomato puree keeps it juicy.

Crisp mustard and tarragon chicken with roasted cherry tomatoes

preparation time 10 minutes / cooking time 30 minutes / serves 4

Toasted bread crumbs are pressed into mustard-tarragon-rubbed chicken breasts and baked until crisp in this cheat's version of fried chicken. The roasted cherry tomatoes provide a tasty accompaniment to serve alongside.

4 boneless, skinless chicken breast halves,
2 tablespoons Dijon mustard
2 shallots, finely chopped
2 tablespoons chopped tarragon leaves, plus whole leaves for garnishing
1½ cups fresh fine bread crumbs, toasted until golden
2 tablespoons olive oil or olive oil spray
9 ounces cherry tomatoes
2 cloves garlic, thickly sliced
boiled baby potatoes, to serve
sea salt
black pepper

Preheat the oven to 400°F. Pound the breasts a little to flatten. Sprinkle the chicken with sea salt and freshly ground black pepper. Mix the mustard, shallots and tarragon together and spread all over the chicken. Roll in the bread crumbs and place on a baking sheet. Drizzle or spray both sides of the chicken with a little of the olive oil.
Bake for 30 minutes or until crisp and browned.

Place the tomatoes and garlic in a small baking dish. Drizzle over the remaining olive oil and season, then place in the oven after the chicken has been baking for 15 minutes. Serve the chicken with the tomatoes and potatoes and garnish with the tarragon.

PREP AHEAD

The chicken can be coated 1 day ahead and refrigerated or frozen. Thaw in the fridge on the day of using.

THE SKINNY

Mustard is a zero-calorie way to add depth but no fat. It also gives the bread crumbs something to stick to so you don't have to go to the trouble of dipping in flour, egg and all of that business.

Chicken, cherry and pistachio pilaf

preparation time 10 minutes / cooking time 35 minutes / serves 4

Traditional pilafs and biryanis take a fair amount of skill and time to get right and are usually made with chunks of lamb. This modern interpretation with aromatic allspice and sweet dried cherries uses quick-cooking chicken breast for a speedy weeknight supper. Serve with Greek-style yogurt.

1½ cups basmati rice
1 tablespoon olive oil
2 large onions, thinly sliced
4 boneless, skinlesss chicken breast
    halves, cut into ¾-inch pieces
3 tablespoons dried cherries,
    roughly chopped
1 teaspoon ground allspice
1 cinnamon stick
2 cups chicken broth
2 tablespoons finely chopped flat-leaf
    (Italian) parsley
2 tablespoons pistachios, chopped
low-fat Greek-style yogurt, to serve
sea salt
black pepper

Rinse the rice three or four times until the water runs clear. Drain and set aside. Heat the olive oil in a large heavy saucepan over medium heat. Add the onions and season with sea salt and freshly ground black pepper. Saute for 12–15 minutes or until very golden and crisp at the edges. Add the chicken, cherries, allspice and cinnamon and saute for 2 minutes or until opaque. Add the rice and broth and bring to a boil. Reduce the heat and simmer, covered with a lid, for 15 minutes. The liquid should be all absorbed. Stir in the parsley, scatter with the pistachios and serve with the yogurt.

PREP AHEAD

The pilaf is best made just before serving.

THE SKINNY

All of the components in this rice dish are virtuous with the exception of the olive oil and pistachios. However, only small amounts of these are used but the taste still comes through.

Chicken with celery salt rub and cider-mustard slaw

preparation time 15 minutes / cooking time 10 minutes / serves 4

Adaptable for both summer and winter eating, the broiled chicken and mustardy cabbage slaw work in either season. Celery salt, a spice that isn't featured often, makes a particularly good rub for chicken or seafood.

4 boneless, skinless chicken breast
  halves
2 teaspoons celery salt
1 teaspoon mild ground chile pepper, or
  to taste
1 teaspoon olive oil
sea salt
black pepper

Cider-mustard slaw
2 tablespoons apple cider vinegar
2 tablespoons whole-grain mustard
1 tablespoon honey
2 tablespoons olive oil
¼ red cabbage (about 1 pound 2
  ounces), finely shredded
2 carrots, finely shredded
1 Granny Smith apple, core removed
  and chopped into matchsticks
1 small white onion, finely chopped

Using a meat mallet, gently pound the chicken breasts so they are an even thickness all over. Mix the spices together with some sea salt and freshly ground black pepper. Rub the olive oil into the chicken, then sprinkle the spices over. Preheat a grill, broiler or grll pan to high.

To make the cider-mustard slaw, mix together the vinegar, mustard, honey and olive oil in a small bowl and season. Place the cabbage, carrots, apple and onion in a large bowl. Pour the dressing over and mix.

Cook the chicken for 4–5 minutes each side and serve with the slaw.

PREP AHEAD

The chicken can be coated and refrigerated 1 day ahead or frozen. Thaw in the fridge on the day of using. The slaw can be made 3 hours before and refrigerated.

THE SKINNY

Spice rubs add dimension to broiled meats without the fat. Honey, vinegar and mustard make a tasty dressing with very little oil.

Jamaican chicken curry

preparation time 10 minutes / cooking time 25 minutes / serves 4

This Caribbean dish is lavished with green chiles, gingerroot and allspice, a trademark trio of Jamaican flavors. The cherry tomatoes and sweet potato add color and extra veg to this aromatic curry.

2 teaspoons olive oil
1 large onion, chopped
2-inch piece of fresh ginger, chopped
1 thumb-sized green chile, finely
  chopped
2 cloves garlic, chopped
1 tablespoon curry powder
½ teaspoon ground allspice
¼ teaspoon sweet paprika
2 cinnamon sticks
1 large sweet potato, peeled and cut into
  1¼-inch chunks
4 boneless, skinless chicken breast
  halves, cut into 1¼-inch chunks
2 cups chicken broth
1 tablespoon white wine vinegar
4 ounces cherry tomatoes
cilantro leaves and steamed basmati
  rice, to serve
sea salt
black pepper

Heat the olive oil in a large skillet over medium heat and saute the onion, ginger, chile and garlic for 5 minutes or until soft. Season with sea salt and freshly ground black pepper and add the spices. Saute for another minute, then add the sweet potato and chicken. Pour in the broth and vinegar. Cook for 15 minutes or until the sweet potato is cooked through. During the last 5 minutes of cooking, add the tomatoes. Scatter with the cilantro and serve with the rice.

PREP AHEAD

The curry can be made 1 day ahead but undercook the sweet potatoes or they will go mushy when reheated. This curry freezes well.

THE SKINNY

Spices, chiles and ginger make this anything but boring. Broth is used instead of coconut milk, because it is less caloric.

Chicken, ginger and green bean hotpot

preparation time 10 minutes / cooking time 20 minutes / serves 4

The ginger quantity sounds large here in this classic Vietnamese braise but it sweetens when cooking and doesn't overpower the dish at all. The Vietnamese add a little sugar to their stir-fries or stews to impart a caramel flavor. When combined with the fish sauce, poached ginger and broth, it's a captivating sauce.

1 tablespoon vegetable oil
2 inch piece of gingerroot,
    cut into julienne
2 cloves garlic, chopped
1 onion, thinly sliced into half moons
2 tablespoons fish sauce
1 tablespoon light brown sugar
1 pound 2 ounces boneless, skinless
    chicken thigh, trimmed of all fat and
    cut in half
1 cup chicken broth
¼ pound green beans, cut into
    1-inch lengths
2 tablespoons chopped cilantro
steamed rice, to serve

Heat the vegetable oil in a saucepan over medium-high heat. Add the ginger, garlic and onion and stir-fry for about 5 minutes or until lightly golden. Add the fish sauce, sugar, chicken and broth. Cover and cook over medium heat for 15 minutes. In the last 2 minutes of cooking, add the green beans. Remove from the heat and stir in half of the cilantro. Serve with the rice and the remaining cilantro scattered on top.

PREP AHEAD

The hotpot can be made 1 day ahead and refrigerated or frozen.

THE SKINNY

The large amounts of ginger and fish sauce infuse the sauce with flavor and make for a very lean dish with little oil.

Italian chicken stew with mushrooms and tomatoes

preparation time 15 minutes / cooking time 35 minutes / serves 4

Dried porcini, once soaked, produce an intense woodsy broth as well as being delicious mushrooms. Both are used in this quick Italian chicken stew for a wonderful rich intensity. Chicken breasts can be used instead, and would make it even lower in fat, but they are not quite as tender as the thighs.

1 cup boiling water
1 ounce dried porcini mushrooms
2 tablespoons olive oil
6 boneless, skinless chicken thighs, trimmed of all fat, cut into bite-sized pieces
1 large yellow onion, thinly sliced into half moons
2 slices prosciutto, chopped
4 clove garlics, chopped
7 ounces button mushrooms, quartered
1 can (14 ounces) whole plum tomatoes
½ cup dry white wine
chopped flat-leaf (Italian) parsley and steamed rice or smashed boiled baby potatoes, to serve
sea salt
black pepper

Pour the boiling water over the porcini mushrooms. Allow to soak for 10 minutes, then drain the liquid into a cup and save for later. Rinse and chop the mushrooms and set aside. Heat a little of the olive oil in a saucepan over medium-high heat. Season the chicken with sea salt and freshly ground black pepper and brown on all sides, about 4 minutes. Remove from the saucepan and add the onion, prosciutto, garlic and remaining olive oil and some seasoning. Saute for 8 minutes or until the onion is golden, then add the fresh mushrooms, porcini mushrooms and tomatoes and saute for 5 minutes. Add the chicken, wine and reserved porcini soaking liquid. Cover and cook over medium-low heat for 15 minutes or until the chicken is tender. Check the seasoning. Add some parsley and serve with rice or potatoes.

PREP AHEAD

The braise can be made 2 days ahead and refrigerated or frozen — simply thaw in the fridge on the day of using.

THE SKINNY

Dried mushrooms and the soaking liquid add flavor to stews without the need for cream. The prosciutto is used in small quantities but still adds a hint of saltiness.

Skinny Meals in Heels

Chicken baked with figs, honey and almonds

preparation time 5 minutes / cooking time 20 minutes / serves 4

When I see fat ripe purple figs in season I like to devise something with them while at their juicy peak. This was a simple Moorish-inspired dish I threw together one evening. The figs break down slightly when cooking, making a jammy sauce for the chicken. It can be made from start to finish in 25 minutes.

1 tablespoon olive oil

2 cloves garlic, sliced

2 tablespoons sherry vinegar

1 tablespoon honey

1 teaspoon ground cinnamon

2 tablespoons flaked almonds, toasted

4 boneless, skinless chicken breast halves

6 ripe purple figs, quartered

2 tablespoons finely chopped flat-leaf (Italian) parsley

steamed couscous, steamed green beans and low-fat Greek-style yogurt, to serve

Preheat the oven to 375°F.

Combine the olive oil, garlic, vinegar, honey, cinnamon and almonds in a bowl and season well. Add the chicken and toss to coat. Transfer to a rimmed baking sheet, scatter with the figs and bake for 20 minutes or until the chicken is just cooked through. Sprinkle with the parsley and serve with the couscous, green beans and yogurt.

PREP AHEAD

The dish can be prepared 4–6 hours ahead and refrigerated, then baked shortly before serving.

THE SKINNY

Roasting or stewing fruit with savory food is a healthy, winning duo. Toasted almonds add crunch and as only a small quantity is used, fat is not a worry.

Ramen noodles with ground turkey, green beans and hoisin sauce

preparation time 10 minutes / cooking time 10 minutes / serves 4

Ground meat suits noodle stir-fries because it absorbs more of the tastes and tucks into the noodles easily. Chile bean paste, a Chinese condiment, is made with fermented soybeans, chile and garlic. It's fiery but has a wonderful addictive taste. A little dollop into a stir-fry adds a "umami" factor. Most supermarkets sell it in the international section. Failing that, you can buy it at an Asian food store, and one jar will last more than a year. Other Asian chile pastes will also substitute well.

¾ cup hoisin sauce

juice of 2 limes

2 tablespoons chile bean paste
   or Chinese chile sauce

1 tablespoon vegetable oil

1 pound 2 ounces ground turkey

3 cloves garlic, chopped

6 ounces green beans, trimmed
   and halved

6 scallions, chopped

7 ounces dried ramen noodles,
   to serve

Bring a large saucepan of salted water to a boil while you get everything ready.

Mix together the hoisin, lime juice and chile sauce in a small bowl. Heat half of the vegetable oil in a wok over high heat, add the turkey and stir-fry, breaking up any clumps with the back of a wooden spoon, until nicely browned. Remove from the wok.

Add the remaining oil to the wok along with the garlic and cook until just golden. Add the beans and scallions. Drop the noodles into the boiling water and cook for 3–4 minutes. Keep stir-frying the vegetables for 1 minute, then add the turkey and hoisin mixture. Stir-fry for 2–3 minutes or until the meat is warmed through and the sauce is sticky. Drain the noodles and serve in bowls with the turkey mixture spooned over.

PREP AHEAD

The sauce and vegetables can be chopped a couple of hours ahead and everything stir-fried just before eating.

THE SKINNY

Chinese condiments like hoisin and chile bean paste add a salty-chile spike to the plain turkey but have little fat.

Veggie

Thai butternut curry with pineapple, beans and tomatoes

preparation time 15 minutes / cooking time 15 minutes / serves 4

Thai red curry paste is a godsend for quick weekday cooking. Butternut squash is a stalwart vegetarian ingredient and especially good in curries. Fresh sweet pineapple and cherry tomatoes elevate this further for a spectacular Thai dinner.

1 tablespoon vegetable oil
3 tablespoons red curry paste
1 can (14 ounces) low-fat coconut milk
½ pound butternut squash, peeled and cut into 1¼ inch chunks
1 tablespoon fish sauce
finely grated zest and juice of 2 limes
¼ pound green beans, trimmed and halved
¼ pound cherry tomatoes
½ small pineapple, peeled, cored and cut into 1¼-inch pieces
cilantro leaves and steamed rice, to serve

Heat the vegetable oil in a saucepan over medium-high heat. Add the curry paste and stir for 2 minutes. Pour in the coconut milk and heat until just boiling. Reduce the heat to a simmer and add the butternut, fish sauce and lime zest and juice. Cook for 10 minutes or until the butternut squash is fork tender. Add the green beans, tomatoes and pineapple and cook for 2 minutes. Sprinkle with the cilantro and serve with the rice.

PREP AHEAD

The curry is best made on the night of serving. It can be frozen but be sure to undercook the butternut squash so it doesn't go mushy when reheating.

THE SKINNY

Thai red curry paste is a delish skinny ingredient to use in curries or as a rub on vegetables, fish or meats.

Whole wheat linguine with broccoli, garlic, chile and lemon

preparation time 5 minutes / cooking time 10 minutes / serves 4

As a poor university student, my staple dinner was garlic spaghetti. It was simply olive oil, garlic and noodles. Parmesan was too dear, so I learned to love this dish on its own with lots of black pepper. My grown-up version has less oil and more goodies thrown in. Nutty garlic, red chile and lashings of lemon are tossed with the linguine and broccoli for an extraordinary but simple pasta.

12 ounces whole wheat linguine
3 tablespoons extra virgin olive oil
1 thumb-sized red chile, thinly sliced, seeds removed
3 cloves garlic, sliced into coins
finely shredded zest and juice of 2 lemons
¾ pound broccolini or purple broccoli, cut into pieces
shredded Parmesan (optional)

Bring a large saucepan of salted water to a boil. Add the pasta and cook until al dente.

Meanwhile, heat the olive oil in a heavy-bottomed skillet over medium-low heat. Add the chile and garlic and cook for 1 minute or until the garlic is golden. Remove from the heat and add the lemon zest and juice.

About 4 minutes before the pasta is done, add the broccoli to the same pan as the pasta. Drain when both are ready. Return to the pan and pour the garlic-chile mixture over. Mix well, season to taste and sprinkle a little Parmesan if desired.

PREP AHEAD

This dish is best made on the night of serving.

THE SKINNY

Adding lemon juice to the garlic oil means you have more flavor without having to use more oil. The lemon also adds a zingy freshness without being too puckery.

Saffron risotto with tomato and spinach

preparation time 10 minutes / **cooking time** 25 minutes / **serves** 4

A good pinch of luxurious saffron makes a weekday meal feel ultra special. A little bag of fresh spinach thrown in at the end makes it a complete meal with vegetables. Be sure to taste your broth before you use it, checking if it is too watery or salty. That's often where risotto goes wrong. If it tastes good to start with, it will produce great risotto.

6½ cups good-quality vegetable broth
1 teaspoon boiling water
1 large pinch of saffron threads, crushed
2 teaspoons olive oil
1 onion, chopped
1¼ cups Arborio rice
½ cup white wine
3 plum tomatoes, seeds removed and
    chopped
7 ounces baby spinach leaves
¼ cup shredded Parmesan
sea salt
black pepper

Heat the broth in a large saucepan until boiling, then reduce to a simmer. Pour the boiling water over the saffron and allow to soak. Heat the olive oil in a separate large heavy-bottomed saucepan over medium heat and saute the onions with a bit of sea salt and freshly ground black pepper for 3–4 minutes or until translucent.

Add the rice and saute for 3 minutes or until the grains are glistening. Pour in the saffron and soaking water and stir a minute, then add the wine. Stir until absorbed. Add one ladleful of broth and stir again until absorbed. Continue this process for about 10–15 minutes or until you have used nearly all of the broth and the rice is cooked but has a tiny bite to it. Add the tomatoes and spinach, check the seasoning and stir again. Sprinkle with the Parmesan.

PREP AHEAD

This dish is best made on the night of serving.

THE SKINNY

Risotto is still delicious and far less gluey without loads of Parmesan. You only need a little for that nutty gorgeous taste.

Mexican beans and rice with avocado salsa

preparation time 10 minutes / cooking time 15 minutes / serves 4–6

Whenever I eat Mexican fast food I like to order a "taco rice bowl." Instead of a tortilla shell, all the same ingredients are put into a bowl. I decided to make it at home as it's so tasty and filling. Here I've played around with the trad "beans and rice", stewing the beans in a garlicky, smoky chipotle, vinegar and honey sauce instead of pork fat. It's served up with warm rice and a chunky avocado salsa.

1¼ cups brown or white basmati rice
1 teaspoon olive oil
3 cloves garlic, chopped
1 small red onion, finely diced
1 can (15 ounces) borlotti or pinto beans, drained and rinsed
3 teaspoons chipotle hot pepper sauce
4¼ tablespoons apple cider vinegar
2 tablespoons honey
lime wedges and chipotle hot pepper sauce, to serve
sea salt
black pepper

Avocado salsa
2 avocados, cut into chunky pieces
1 small red onion, finely diced
3 tablespoons chopped cilantro
juice of 1 lime

Place the rice in a large saucepan and cover with 2¾ inches water. Bring to a boil, then reduce the heat and simmer for 15–20 minutes or until al dente. Drain, then return to the saucepan. Cover with a lid to keep warm until using.

Heat the olive oil in a heavy-bottomed saucepan over medium heat. Add the garlic and onion and cook for 5 minutes or until golden. Add the beans, chipotle sauce, vinegar, honey and some sea salt and freshly ground black pepper. Saute for 5 minutes or until the flavors come together.

To make the avocado salsa, mix the avocado, onion, cilantro and lime juice together.

Divide the rice among plates, spoon the beans over and top with the salsa. Serve with the lime wedges and hot pepper sauce.

PREP AHEAD

The bean mixture can be made 1 day ahead and refrigerated or frozen — just thaw in the fridge on the day of using. Make the salsa just before serving to keep the color of the avocado green.

THE SKINNY

Beans, when combined with rice, make a complete protein keeping you full. The garlic, vinegar and chilli keep the sauce skinny without saturated fat or excess oil.

Risotto primavera

preparation time 10 minutes / cooking time 25 minutes / serves 4

This classic green and orange speckled risotto is a slimmer version of the retro seventies cream-laden recipe, but being skinny doesn't mean it's lost any of its impressiveness.

6½ cups good-quality vegetable broth
1 tablespoon olive oil
1 onion, finely chopped
2 large carrots, cut into ½-inch dice
2 zucchini, cut into ½-inch dice
1¼ cups Arborio rice
¾ cup shelled fresh or frozen peas
6 scallions, finely chopped
4 tablespoons shredded Parmesan
sea salt
black pepper

Heat the broth in a large saucepan until boiling, then reduce to a simmer. Heat the olive oil in a separate large heavy-bottomed saucepan over medium heat and saute the onion, carrot and zucchini along with some sea salt and freshly ground black pepper for 3–4 minutes or until the onion is translucent.

Add the rice and saute for 3 minutes or until the grains are glistening. Add one ladleful of broth and stir until absorbed. Continue this process for about 15 minutes or until you have used nearly all of the broth and the rice is cooked but has a tiny bite to it. About 5 minutes before the rice is ready, add the peas and scallions. Serve each portion with a tablespoon of Parmesan.

PREP AHEAD

This is best made on the night of serving.

THE SKINNY

Risotto is mistakenly thought of as fattening but it is quite healthy and if the Parmesan is kept to a minimum (as it is here — only 1 tablespoon per person), it's pretty slim. This is a great all-in-one dish with three of your five-a-day vegetables.

Polenta with roasted eggplant, tomato and olive sauce

preparation time 15 minutes / cooking time 30 minutes / serves 4

Creamy polenta (minus the cream and butter) is topped with a garlicky tomato and olive sauce and chunks of golden roasted eggplant for an Italian meatless meal. You could also use roasted butternut squash and crisp leaves of sage if you're not an eggplant lover.

2 eggplant, cut into 1¼-inch chunks
2 tablespoons olive oil
3 cloves garlic, chopped
1 large pinch of chile flakes
1 can (14 ounces) whole plum tomatoes
8 oil-cured black olives, pitted
   and halved
4 cups vegetable broth
1¼ cups instant polenta
¼ cup shredded Parmesan
4 handfuls arugula leaves,
   to serve
sea salt
black pepper

Preheat the oven to 375°F. Toss the eggplant with 1 tablespoon of the olive oil. Season well with sea salt and freshly ground black pepper and spread out on a large baking sheet. Roast for 25 minutes or until golden.

Heat the remaining olive oil in a saucepan over medium heat. Add the garlic and chile flakes and saute for 2 minutes or until golden. Add the tomatoes, a good teaspoon of salt and cook for 10 minutes or until thickened. Add the olives in the last 5 minutes of cooking. Reduce the heat to low and keep warm.

Heat the broth in a saucepan. When it comes to a boil, slowly add the polenta. Stir until it has thickened, 1–2 minutes. Add half of the Parmesan and stir again. Serve up four bowls with the polenta. Pour some warm tomato and olive sauce over and scatter the roasted eggplant on top. Place a handful of arugula on each and sprinkle with the remaining Parmesan.

PREP AHEAD

This dish is best made on the night of serving.

THE SKINNY

The polenta has been stripped down here and made without the usual butter or cream, but it still tastes very good lushed up with broth and Parmesan.

Roasted harissa vegetables with kale, chile and ginger pilaf

preparation time 15 minutes / cooking time 30 minutes / serves 4

Harissa works as an instant rub for these roasted vegetables served up with a gingerroot and kale pilaf and Greek-style yogurt. Any vegetables can be used here, such as eggplant or zucchini.

1 butternut squash (about 2 ¼ pounds, peeled and cut into 1¼-inch chunks
2 red onions, quartered
2 red bell peppers, cut into 1¼-inch pieces
1–2 tablespoons harissa paste, or to taste
low-fat Greek-style yogurt, to serve
sea salt
black pepper

Kale, ginger and chile pilaf
1 tablespoon olive oil
1 onion, thinly sliced
2 clove garlics, chopped
1¼-inch piece of ginger, peeled and finely chopped
1 thumb-sized red chile, seeds removed and sliced
¼ pound kale or other greens, chopped
1 cup basmati rice
2 cups vegetable broth

Preheat the oven to 400°F. Place the butternut squash, onions and peppers on a large baking sheet or two smaller ones. Toss them with the harissa and season with sea salt and freshly ground black pepper. Roast for 30 minutes or until golden and tender.

Meanwhile, make the kale, ginger and chile pilaf. Heat the olive oil in a saucepan over medium heat, add the onion, garlic, ginger and chile and season. Saute for 5 minutes or until the onion is translucent. Add the kale, rice and broth. Bring to a boil, reduce the heat to low, cover with a lid and cook for 8 minutes or until tender. Serve with the roasted vegetables and some yogurt alongside.

PREP AHEAD

This is best made on the night of serving.

THE SKINNY

Four servings of vegetables make this sing with health, but more importantly it's an aromatic and delicious dish spiked with ginger and chile.

Sweet and sour red lentil dhal with roasted eggplant

preparation time 10 minutes / cooking time 30 minutes / serves 4

Indian dhal is cheap as chips, good for you and full of solace. Golden chunks of roasted eggplant add a meaty texture, but you can substitute any vegetable you like, such as roasted winter-squash, blanched green beans or even diced carrots.

1 eggplant, cut into 1¼ inch chunks
3 tablespoons vegetable oil
1 cup red lentils
1 teaspoon ground turmeric
4 cups vegetable broth or water
1 yellow onion, thinly sliced
2 cloves garlic, finely chopped
1 tablespoon finely grated fresh ginger
2 teaspoons garam masala
  or curry powder
½ cup tamarind puree
steamed basmati rice, lime pickle or
  chutney and cilantro leaves, to serve
sea salt
black pepper

Preheat the oven to 375°F.
Toss the eggplant chunks with 1 tablespoon of the vegetable oil and season well with sea salt and freshly ground black pepper. Roast for 20 minutes or until golden.

Meanwhile, rinse the lentils and place in a saucepan. Add the turmeric and broth and season with salt. Bring to a boil over high heat and cook for 15 minutes or until very soft. Skim any foam that may form on the top.

Heat the remaining vegetable oil in a heavy-bottomed skillet over medium heat. Add the onion, garlic and ginger, season and cook for 5 minutes or until golden. Add the garam masala and saute for 2 minutes. Add the tamarind puree and the cooked lentils and simmer for 5 minutes.

Serve with the eggplant, rice and lime pickle or chutney with the cilantro scattered over.

PREP AHEAD

The dhal can be made up to 2 days ahead and refrigerated. It may need thinning out with a bit of broth or water. It can also be frozen.

THE SKINNY

Eaten with rice, lentils make a complete protein. They require hardly any oil to cook and the ginger, garlic, onion and spice give them a kick.

Zucchini, tomato and onion gratin with crisp bread crumbs

preparation time 15 minutes / cooking time 40 minutes / serves 4

Growing up in Wisconsin, my dad, Leo, had a bursting vegetable garden. At the end of summer, we had crate upon crate of zucchini. I would secretly curse them because my sisters and I would have to can, pickle and cook them for days. This was one of my mother's magical recipes on how to use them up. The slices are stewed in a sweet tomato-onion sauce and the Parmesan bread crumbs (my addition) add some crunch.

3 tablespoons olive oil
2 large yellow onions, thinly sliced
   into half moons
3 cloves garlic, chopped
1 large pinch of chile flakes
1 can (14 ounces) whole plum tomatoes
4 zucchini, cut into ⅛-inch-thick slices
2 handfuls fresh sourdough bread
   crumbs
2 tablespoons shredded Parmesan
sea salt
black pepper

Preheat the oven to 375°F/Gas 5. Heat 2 tablespoons of the olive oil in a large saucepan over medium-high heat. Add the onion, garlic and chile flakes, season with sea salt and freshly ground black pepper and saute for 10 minutes or until light golden. Add the tomatoes and break up with a spoon. Cook for 10 minutes or until thick. Add the zucchini and pour into a 12 x 9-inch baking dish. Toss the bread crumbs with the remaining olive oil and Parmesan and season. Spread over the top of the zucchini mixture and bake for 20 minutes or until crisp and golden.

PREP AHEAD

The entire gratin can be made 4 hours ahead and refrigerated, then reheated. Otherwise prepare it 2 hours ahead and bake before eating.

THE SKINNY

Only a small amount of Parmesan is used in the bread crumbs to add more taste. Since the zucchini are baked in the tomato sauce, very little oil is used.

Squid ink spaghetti with fennel, cherry tomatoes and basil

preparation time 10 minutes / cooking time 20 minutes / serves 4

Squid ink spaghetti doesn't really taste that much different from plain pasta but its noir color is striking. With some white fennel, basil and cherry tomatoes, it's even more stunning. But more important than its beauty, it's a lovely dish to devour. Substitute regular pasta if you like.

2 tablespoons extra virgin olive oil
4 cloves garlic, finely chopped
1 large pinch of chile flakes
4 small fennel bulbs, cores removed, thinly sliced and chopped
9 ounces cherry tomatoes, halved
14 ounces dried squid ink spaghetti
1 small handful basil leaves, torn
2 tablespoons shredded Parmesan
sea salt
black pepper

Heat the olive oil in a large skillet over medium heat, add the garlic, chile and fennel. Season well with sea salt and freshly ground black pepper and saute for 15 minutes or until softened. Add the tomato, season again and cook for 5 minutes or until the tomatoes break down a bit.

Meanwhile, cook the pasta in a large saucepan of salted boiling water until al dente, then drain. Add the drained pasta and the basil to the tomato sauce. Serve in bowls with Parmesan scattered over.

PREP AHEAD

This is best made on the night of serving.

THE SKINNY

These are all lean tasty ingredients with little fat. Just a small sprinkling of Parmesan gives you the nutty taste of the cheese without copious calories. For more protein, throw some white crabmeat or shrimp into the sauce just when it's nearly ready.

Cilantro potato cakes with mango chutney

preparation time 15 minutes / **cooking time** 20 minutes / **serves** 4

You won't be yearning for meat with these spice-kissed potato cakes studded with scallion, lemon zest and bits of melty cheese. They taste fried with their crisp bread crumbs but are very chaste indeed.

1 pound 2 ounces baking potatoes, peeled
1 egg, separated
1 handful cilantro leaves, chopped
6 small scallions, thinly sliced
grated zest of 1 lemon
3 ounces low-fat Cheddar, shredded
1 thumb-sized red chile, seeds removed and chopped
¾ cup fine dried bread crumbs, toasted
1 tablespoon vegetable oil
mango chutney and green salad, to serve
sea salt
black pepper

Cook the potatoes in salted boiling water until they start to fall apart. Drain and place back in the warm pan to dry out for a few minutes. Mash the potato with the egg yolk, cilantro and scallions. Season with sea salt and freshly ground black pepper and mix in the lemon zest, Cheddar and chile. Shape into 8 cakes.

Place the egg white in a bowl and whisk until foamy. Place the bread crumbs on a plate. Dip the cakes in the eggwhite, allow the excess to drain off, then coat in the bread crumbs, pressing to adhere well. Place on a baking sheet lined with parchment paper, cover and refrigerate until using.

Heat the vegetable oil in a large heavy-bottomed nonstick skillet over medium heat. Cook the cakes in batches for 2–3 minutes each side or until golden and heated through. Serve with the chutney and salad.

PREP AHEAD

The cakes can be made 1 day ahead and refrigerated or frozen — thaw in the fridge. Pan-fry just before you want to eat them.

THE SKINNY

Vegetable cakes don't have to be hugely caloric if you use a good heavy-bottomed nonstick skillet. It will conduct the heat better and you won't need as much oil. Just keep the temperature low so that they brown slowly.

Broiled wasabi salmon with chunky cucumber and poppyseed salad

preparation time 10 minutes / cooking time 5 minutes / serves 4

Spicy wasabi makes a glaze for grilled fish in the bat of an eye. The cucumber salad, with its crunchy poppy seeds, chile and rice vinegar dressing, creates a refreshing side.

4 skin-on salmon fillets (4 to 5 ounces each)
1 teaspoon vegetable oil
2 tablespoons wasabi paste
1 European cucumber
1 thumb-sized red chile, cut into rounds
2 tablespoons rice vinegar
1 tablespoon superfine sugar
1 tablespoon poppyseeds
steamed rice, to serve
sea salt
black pepper

Rub both sides of the salmon with a tiny bit of the vegetable oil and then the wasabi paste. Halve the cucumber lengthwise and remove the seeds. Cut the cucumber diagonally into 1½-inch chunks and place in a bowl. Add the chile, vinegar, sugar, poppyseeds, and a bit of sea salt and freshly ground black pepper. Mix to disslove the sugar and salt.

Preheat the broiler to high. Cook the salmon fillets, skin side down, without turning for 5–6 minutes, depending on their thickness. Serve with the salad and the steamed rice.

PREP AHEAD

You can coat the fish 1 day ahead and refrigerate or freeze. Thaw in the refrigerator before cooking. Mix the salad just before eating.

THE SKINNY

Wasabi, like other Asian pastes, makes a zero-fat glaze and complements salmon's rich character.

Spaghetti with red clam sauce and gremolata

preparation time 10 minutes / soaking time 1 hour / cooking time 15 minutes / serves 4

Some red clam sauces have a long list of ingredients, but this one is dead simple with the clams steamed right on top of the garlicky tomato sauce. It all relies on getting little baby clams that are tender and delicate. The bigger ones are too rubbery. A sharp lemon and parsley gremolata is sprinkled on top for a knockout pasta.

1 pound 5 ounces baby clams
1 tablespoon sea salt
1 tablespoon olive oil
2 anchovy fillets, rinsed
1 large pinch of chile flakes
4 clove garlics, chopped
3 cans (14 ounces each) whole plum
   tomatoes
14 ounces spaghetti
finely grated zest of 1 lemon
2 tablespoons chopped flat-leaf
   (Italian) parsley

Cover the clams with water, add the salt and refrigerate for 1 hour, agitating the clams regularly. This helps them to "burp up" any sand they have inside.

Heat the olive oil in a large saucepan with a fitted lid over medium heat. Add the anchovy fillets, chile and garlic and saute for 2 minutes or until golden. Add the tomatoes and break up with a spoon. Cook for 10 minutes or until slightly thickened and reduced. Season to taste.

Cook the pasta in salted boiling water until al dente. In the last 5 minutes of the pasta cooking, add the clams to the tomato sauce, keeping them mostly on top of the sauce, cover with the lid and steam until they open.

Drain the pasta and add to the tomato sauce. Cook for a few minutes, then add the lemon zest and parsley and toss to combine.

PREP AHEAD

This is best made on the night of serving.

THE SKINNY

Shellfish like clams are packed with flavorful juices that don't add any calories. The lemon and parsley cut through the richness, keeping the dish fresh and light.

Shrimp tacos with black beans and pickled jalapeño salsa

preparation time 15 minutes / cooking time 10 minutes / serves 4

Fresh tomato salsa with pickled jalapeños will make any taco or Mexican dish infinitely better. Substitute firm white fish fillets or chicken in place of the shrimp if you like. Roll everything up in a soft tortilla or make the crisp oven-baked ones (see page 109).

1 pound 2 ounces large peeled shrimp, butterflied (split and flattened)
1 teaspoon ground cumin
1 teaspoon chili powder
2 cans (15 ounces each) black beans, drained and rinsed
fresh corn or flour tortillas , low-fat
1 teaspoon vegetable oil
1 lime, halved
Greek-style yogurt, chopped cilantro and hot-pepper sauce, to serve

Jalapeño salsa
1 small red onion, finely diced
2 limes, one juiced and the other halved
2 tablespoons chopped pickled jalapeños or 1 chopped green chile
1 handful cilantro leaves, chopped
½ pound cherry tomatoes, quartered
sea salt
black pepper

To make the jalapeño salsa, place the onion in a bowl and pour in the lime juice. Allow to sit for 5 minutes, then add the pickled jalapeños, cilantro and tomato. Season with sea salt and freshly ground black pepper and set aside.

Preheat the oven to 400°F.

Mix the shrimp with the spices and season.

Heat the beans in a saucepan over low heat, slightly mashing them.

Warm the tortillas in foil in the oven for 5 minutes.

Heat the vegetable oil in a large skillet over high heat. Cook the shrimp about 1 minute each side, then squeeze the lime halves over them.

To serve, spoon some of the black beans over each tortilla, top with the shrimp, salsa, yogurt, some cilantro and a good dash of hot pepper sauce.

PREP AHEAD

The salsa can be made a couple of hours ahead. The rest should be done just before serving.

THE SKINNY

All the ingredients here are virtuous. Refried beans, which normally entail lard, are replaced with warm black beans, and Greek-style yogurt stands in for the sour cream.

Bengali salmon parcels with mustard-yogurt paste

preparation time 15 minutes / cooking time 10 minutes / serves 4

Any firm fish will work with this simple Indian yogurt marinade of gingerroot, green chiles and whole-grain mustard. Traditionally it's a recipe that involves mustard oil but it's a tricky ingredient to find so I've devised my own interpretation. Eat with fragrant basmati rice and fat wedges of lemon to squeeze over everything.

4 skinless salmon fillets (4 to 5 ounces each)

1 teaspoon ground turmeric

1 teaspoon ground cumin

1¼-inch piece of fresh ginger, peeled and sliced

1 clove garlic

1 small handful cilantro, chopped

2 thumb-sized green chiles, seeds removed and sliced

2 tablespoons whole-grain mustard

7 ounces low-fat Greek-style yogurt, plus extra to serve

steamed basmati rice and lemon wedges, to serve

sea salt

black pepper

Preheat a grill to high or the oven to 400°F. Rub the salmon with the turmeric and cumin then season with sea salt and freshly ground black pepper. Place the ginger, garlic, cilantro and nearly all of the chiles in a food processor and process until finely chopped. Add the mustard, half of the yogurt and some sea salt and pulse to combine.

Prepare four doubled sheets of foil. Spread the paste on both sides of the fish pieces. Place a piece on one half of a sheet, then bring the other half over and fold in the sides to make a parcel and seal. Repeat with the remaining fish.

Cook the parcels for 8–10 minutes. Open one to check if the fish is done; if not, seal up again and give it another minute or two. For thicker fish, you may need a few more minutes. Serve with the rice, yogurt and lemon wedges.

PREP AHEAD

The fish can be marinated 1 day ahead and refrigerated or frozen — simply thaw in the fridge the day before.

THE SKINNY

Low-fat Greek-style yogurt and mustard are the star skinny ingredients in this Indian marinade and they're all guilt-free.

Stir-fried fish with dill and rice noodles

preparation time 15 minutes / cooking time 5 minutes / serves 4

This delicious Vietnamese specialty is called *cha ca*. An entire street in Hanoi is dedicated to restaurants that specialize in it. My family and I visited there quite a few times on our trip. The turmeric and garlic–marinated fish is stir-fried with copious amounts of dill including the stalks. It's eaten over rice noodles with pickled red chiles, herbs and crushed peanuts and is utterly divine. Totally simple and amazing. Be sure to use fish that is thick and non-flaky and that can withstand stir-frying.

1 small onion, coarsely shredded

2 cloves garlic, chopped

1 inch piece of ginger, finely chopped

2 teaspoons ground turmeric

2 tablespoons fish sauce

2 tablespoons peanut oil

2 pounds skinless, red snapper, monk-fish or tilapia fillets, cut into 1½-inch chunks

7 ounces dried rice vermicelli noodles

6 scallions, thinly sliced

⅔ cup roughly chopped dill stalks and leaves

chopped roasted peanuts, cilantro sprigs, sliced red chile marinated in rice vinegar and lime wedges, to serve

Combine the onion, garlic, ginger, turmeric, fish sauce and 1 teaspoon of the peanut oil in a bowl. Mix well, then add the fish and allow to marinate for 10 minutes.

Meanwhile, place the noodles in a large bowl and cover with boiling water. Leave to sit for about 5 minutes or until tender, then drain.

Heat the remaining peanut oil in a large wok over high heat. Add the scallions and dill and cook for 1 minute, then add the fish mixture. Stir-fry for 3–4 minutes or until the fish is cooked through.

Divide the noodles among bowls and serve the fish on top with its juices spooned over. Serve with a small sprinkling of peanuts, the cilantro, chile vinegar and lime wedges.

PREP AHEAD

The fish can be marinated up to 3 hours before or frozen in the marinade.

THE SKINNY

The fresh herbs, turmeric and fish sauce provide punch without fat and the rice noodles keep this dish filling.

Sicilian fish and couscous stew

preparation time 10 minutes / **cooking time** 20 minutes / **serves** 4

In Trapani, Sicily, where this fish stew was created, they throw in whole fish. Although the heads, tails and bones add flavor to the base, they aren't much fun to fish out. This is my modern interpretation but it is still reminiscent of the delicious seaside stew.

4 ounces fregola or regular couscous

2 tablespoons olive oil

2 onions, thinly sliced

4 celery ribs, thinly sliced

4 cloves garlic, sliced

1 anchovy fillet

1 pinch of chile flakes

4 large plum tomatoes, seeds removed and diced

1 cup white wine

3 ¼ cups vegetable broth

4 red mullet or other firm white fish fillets (4 to 5 ounces each)

finely grated zest of 1 lemon

2 tablespoons chopped flat-leaf (Italian) parsley

If using fregola, cook it in salted boiling water for about 5 minutes or until al dente. Drain and set aside. If using regular couscous, mix it with the ½ cup boiling water, season with sea salt and freshly ground black pepper, cover and allow to sit.

Heat the olive oil in a large saucepan over medium heat, add the onions, celery, garlic, anchovy fillet and chile flakes, season and saute for 10 minutes or until light golden. Add the tomato and saute for another couple of minutes. Pour in the wine and broth and bring to a boil. Reduce the heat to a simmer and add the fish. Cover with a lid and cook for 5 minutes or until the fish is cooked.

If using fregola, add it to the saucepan. If using couscous, break it up with your fingers and add it to the pan. Divide among large bowls and sprinkle with the lemon zest and parsley.

PREP AHEAD

The stew base and boiled fregola can be prepared 1 day ahead and refrigerated. Add the fish and reheat the stew base just before serving.

THE SKINNY

A tomato base for fish is tasty and uses very little oil.

Seared scallops with smashed potatoes and lemon-chile sauce

preparation time 10 minutes / cooking time 15 minutes / serves 4

I made this dish for my friend Sarah Birks who christened it "healthy posh nosh." If bought in season, scallops won't be expensive. Not just for special occasions, they make an incredibly fast and light dinner. Smashed potatoes mixed with greens are the base for these decadent molluscs and a warm lemon, caper and chile dressing brings it all together.

1 pound 2 ounces baby potatoes
¼ pound Tuscan black kale (cavolo nero) or savoy cabbage, center ribs discarded, leaves thinly sliced
3 tablespoons extra virgin olive oil
1 tablespoon baby capers, rinsed
3 cloves garlic, thinly sliced
2 thumb-sized red chiles, seeds removed and sliced
juice of 1 lemon
12 large scallops
sea salt
black pepper

Cook the potatoes in salted boiling water for 10 minutes. Add the kale in the last 2–3 minutes. Drain and place back in the saucepan. Drizzle with 1 teaspoon of the oil, season with sea salt and roughly mash together. Keep warm while you make the sauce and cook the scallops.

Heat 2 tablespoons of the olive oil in a small skillet over medium-high heat. Add the capers, garlic and chiles and saute for 1–2 minutes or until golden. Remove from the heat and add the lemon juice. Place back on the heat and reduce for 1 minute.

Heat the remaining olive oil in a heavy-bottomed skillet over high heat. When very hot, add the scallops, season with sea salt and freshly ground black pepper and sear for 1 minute each side or until golden brown but not cooked all the way through (scallops are best cooked this way but cook them through if you like). Remove and serve with the potatoes and sauce poured over.

PREP AHEAD

The sauce and potatoes can be made a couple of hours ahead. Sear the scallops at the last minute.

THE SKINNY

The lemon in the sauce keeps it skinny without extra oil and cuts through the richness of the scallops. When lemon juice is allowed to sizzle in the skillet, it loses its acidity.

Grilled tuna steaks with ponzu sauce and Granny Smith apple salad

preparation time 10 minutes / cooking time 5 minutes / serves 4

Ponzu sauce is a Japanese dipping sauce, that consists of soy sauce, citrus juice and sugar. It's mainly used as a condiment for fried food, but I love it for dipping and as a marinade or tart dressing. Grilled tuna and the tart apple and celery salad soak up the tangy ginger-infused sauce for a winning trio.

4½ tablespoons Japanese soy sauce

juice of 2 limes

1 tablespoon superfine sugar

4 tuna steaks (4 to 5 ounces each)

1 tablespoon finely chopped fresh ginger

1 teaspoon vegetable oil

steamed rice, to serve

sea salt

black pepper

Granny Smith salad

2 Granny Smith apples, cores removed
  and cut into matchsticks

4 handfuls watercress sprigs

2 celery ribs, cut into thin matchsticks

4 scallions, thinly sliced

Mix together the soy, nearly all of the lime juice (reserving a little for the salad) and the sugar. Spoon a bit over the tuna and rub it into the flesh, along with the ginger and vegetable oil. Season with sea salt and freshly ground black pepper. Reserve the remaining sauce for serving.

Preheat a grill, broiler or grill pan to high.

To make the salad, mix the apple with the reserved lime juice and toss with the watercress, celery and scallions.

Cook the tuna for 1–1½ minutes each side, keeping the center fairly rare. Serve with the salad and drizzle with the sauce. Serve with the rice.

PREP AHEAD

The ponzu sauce can be made the day before. Everything else should be done shortly before eating.

THE SKINNY

The lime counters the saltiness of the soy in the ponzu sauce for the tuna and also makes a slim dressing for the salad.

Salmon and horseradish pies with crisp potato crust

preparation time 20 minutes / cooking time 35 minutes / serves 4

One wouldn't necessarily expect to find a pie of any sort in a healthy food cookbook but this fish pie just goes to show that anything is possible. A golden potato crust replaces the traditional pastry, and scallion, horseradish, dill and lemon zest bolster the white sauce for a full-on flavored pie. Be sure to use flaky smoked fillets, not the thinly sliced type.

2–3 red-skinned potatoes, scrubbed and cut into ¼-inch slices
1 ounce unsalted butter
1 large bunch scallions, chopped
3 tablespoons all-purpose flour
3 cups fat-free milk
2 tablespoons prepared horseradish, or to taste
2 tablespoons chopped dill
finely grated zest of 1 lemon
14 ounces hot-smoked salmon or trout, skin and bones removed, flesh broken into big chunks
olive oil spray
sea salt
black pepper

Preheat the oven to 400°F.

Bring a saucepan of salted water to a boil. Drop in the potato slices and cook for 3 minutes or until just al dente. Drain well and lay out on a sheet lined with a kitchen towel to dry.

Melt the butter in a saucepan over medium–low heat. Add the scallion and saute for 2 minutes. Whisk in the flour and cook for 1 minute. Season with sea salt and freshly ground black pepper and whisk in the milk and horseradish. Bring to a boil and allow to thicken for a couple of minutes, then add a good teaspoon of salt, the dill, lemon zest and fish.

Pour into four 10-ounce capacity porcelain ramekins. Layer the potatoes over, slightly overlapping like fish scales and spray with the oil. Place on a baking sheet, season and bake for 20–25 minutes or until golden and bubbly.

PREP AHEAD

The pie mixture can be made 1 day ahead and refrigerated or frozen. If freezing, leave the potatoes off since they don't freeze well. Thaw the pies in the refrigerator on the day of cooking.

THE SKINNY

Pot pies don't have to be calorie crushers. The white sauce is nice and thick, but using fat-free milk keeps it light but still provides a thick sauce. Lemon zest and horseradish pump it full of flavor and counter the rich fish.

Fish roast with potato, fennel and tomato-olive vinaigrette

preparation time 10 minutes / cooking time 40 minutes / serves 4

For so little effort, there is a lot of payback here. Whack the potato and fish in the oven to roast then spoon the tomato, olive and shallot dressing over it. It's important to use oil-cured olives, not brine cured (like Kalamata) as they are too salty and overpower the taste of the other ingredients.

1 pound 2 ounces Yukon Gold potatoes, scrubbed and cut into ½-inch slices
4 small fennel bulbs, cores removed and thickly sliced
1 tablespoon extra virgin olive oil
4 salmon, halibut, tilapia or other fish fillets (4 to 5 ounces each)
1 teaspoon fennel seeds, slightly crushed
sea salt
black pepper

Tomato-olive vinaigrette
1 tablespoon white balsamic or white wine vinegar
2 shallots, thinly sliced
2 tablespoons extra virgin olive oil
2 plum tomatoes, seeds removed and diced
15 oil-cured black olives, pitted and roughly chopped

Preheat the oven to 400°F.

Arrange the potato and fennel slices in a single layer on a large baking sheet. Drizzle with the olive oil and season with sea salt and freshly ground black pepper. Bake for 30 minutes or until golden and nearly cooked through, then place the fish on top and sprinkle with the fennel seeds and more seasoning. Bake for another 10 minutes or until the fish is cooked.

Meanwhile, make the tomato-olive vinaigrette. Pour the vinegar over the shallots in a bowl and allow to sit for a few minutes, then add the olive oil, tomatoes and olives and season. Mix well and set aside.

Serve the potato, fennel and fish bake with the vinaigrette spooned over.

PREP AHEAD

This meal is best made just before eating.

THE SKINNY

Roasting vegetables makes them crisp but very low in fat. The vinaigrette is a tasty skinny sauce to replace mayonnaise or crème fraîche–based sauces.

Southern red rice shrimp with celery and tomatoes

preparation time 15 minutes / cooking time 30 minutes / serves 4

Creole food relies on staple spices like bay, celery salt and cayenne, which make their cuisine so addictive. One of my favorite dishes is jambalaya, which has a hefty list of ingredients. This is a much simpler, leaner rendition but just as mouthwatering.

3 slices bacon, chopped
1 tablespoon olive oil
1 large yellow onion, finely chopped
1 red bell pepper, chopped into ¾-inch pieces
3 celery ribs, cut into ¾-inch-thick slices
1 teaspoon celery salt
4 fresh bay leaves
1 can (14 ounces) whole plum tomatoes
1¼ cups basmati rice
2 ¾ cups chicken broth
14 ounces raw large shrimp, peeled and deveined
chopped flat-leaf (Italian) parsley and lemon wedges, to serve

Cook the bacon in a heavy-bottomed saucepan over high heat for 5 minutes or until crisp. Remove, drain on paper towels and discard the fat. Add the olive oil to the saucepan, along with the onion, bell pepper, celery and celery salt and cook over medium heat for 8–10 minutes or until soft. Add the bay leaves, tomatoes and rice and cook for another minute. Pour in the broth, cover with a lid, reduce the heat to low and cook for 10 minutes. Add the shrimp and cook for 5 minutes. Sprinkle with the parsley and serve with the lemon wedges.

PREP AHEAD

This dish is best made just before eating.

THE SKINNY

Yes there is a tiny amount of bacon here but only 3 slices. That's enough to impart a smoky flavor. Turkey bacon, which is very low in fat, can also be used.

Steamed lemon-ginger fish with sticky teriyaki sauce

preparation time 15 minutes / cooking time 15 minutes / serves 4

This Japanese-inspired hotpot is a snap to put together. The fish is placed right on top of the cooking rice and showered with ginger, chiles and lemon. A thickened teriyaki sauce is poured over just before eating.

1¼ cups basmati rice

2 cups water

4 red snapper, tilapia or other fish fillets
(4 to 5 ounces each)

1¼ inch piece of fresh ginger,
grated

1 thumb-sized red chile, seeds removed
and sliced

1 lemon, halved and one-half
thinly sliced

sliced scallions, to garnish

sea salt

black pepper

Sticky teriyaki sauce

7 tablespoons Japanese soy sauce

7 tablespoons mirin

juice of ½ lemon

3 tablespoons sugar

To make the sticky teriyaki sauce, place all the ingredients in a saucepan and bring to a boil. Simmer for 5 minutes or until slightly syrupy. Remove and set aside.

Rinse the rice in a saucepan 2–3 times or until the water runs clear. Drain and cover with the two cups water. Bring to a boil, then reduce the heat to a simmer and cook for about 5 minutes. When the rice has absorbed three-quarters of the water, place the fish fillets on top. Squeeze the lemon half over each piece of fish, then top with the ginger, chile and a slice of lemon. Season with sea salt and freshly ground black pepper, cover with a lid and cook for about 5 minutes or until the fish is cooked.

To serve drizzle the sauce over the fish and rice and garnish with scallions.

PREP AHEAD

The sauce can be made 1 day ahead and refrigerated. Thin with a bit of water when reheating.

THE SKINNY

Steaming is the perfect treatment for delicate fish and this entire dish doesn't require any oil.

Weekend Cooking

Lamb kleftiko

preparation time 10 minutes / cooking time 2½–3 hours / serves 4

All of these ingredients get wrapped up in a large parcel to steam and slow-roast for hours. It's little effort for a high return. Pop it in the oven, go for a walk and leave it to cook. When you open it, the meat flakes apart and the lemons are almost caramelized. Serve it with steamed rice or roasted chunky potatoes.

4½ pounds boneless lamb leg or
    shoulder, trimmed of all external fat
1⅔ tablespoons olive oil
8 cloves garlic, halved
1 teaspoon ground cinnamon
1 tablespoon dried wild oregano
1 lemon, zest removed in wide strips
    and juiced
2 plum tomatoes, quartered
½ cup white wine
Greek-style yogurt and steamed rice
    or potatoes, to serve
sea salt
black pepper

Preheat the oven to 315°F. Cut the lamb into 5 inch pieces and season with sea salt and freshly ground black pepper. Heat the olive oil in a large skillet over high heat until very hot. Sear the lamb on both sides until nicely browned. Using a pointy knife, make incisions in the lamb and push the garlic into the slits.

Tear off two sheets of foil about 4 feet long and place inside a roasting pan. Bring up the sides as if making a shallow bowl. Place the lamb in the center and add the cinnamon, oregano, lemon zest and juice, tomatoes and wine. Season again, then fold over the edges of the foil to seal completely; make sure there is room for air to circulate but also that the foil is tight enough so the lamb steams as it cooks. Check the meat after 2½ hours and if it isn't meltingly tender, put it back in the oven for another 30 minutes. If it's dry, add a tiny bit more wine but it shouldn't need it. Serve with yogurt and rice or potatoes.

PREP AHEAD

The meat can be seared, cooled, sealed up and refrigerated on the morning of serving, ready to roast later.

THE SKINNY

Slow-roasting requires hardly any oil.
If there is fat marbling in the meat it will melt out while cooking, leaving fork-tender flesh.

Skinny *Meals in Heels*

Poulet au pot with salsa verde

preparation time 15 minutes / **cooking time** 1½ hours / **serves** 4–6

This classic French dish is about as virtuous as food gets, but it is utterly divine. The chicken cooks up snowy white and the vegetables so pure, it's a wonder why we don't poach food more often. Piquant herb salsa verde is served up alongside to drizzle over. Wafts of chicken broth will perfume your kitchen while it slowly bubbles away.

1 whole chicken (3¾ pounds)
1 onion, studded with 4 whole cloves
1 bouquet garni (thyme and parsley
   sprigs and a bay leaf tied together
   in a bundle)
4 large carrots, halved
2 leeks, cut into 4-inch pieces
3 small turnips, halved
cooked Puy (French) lentils,
   to serve (optional)

Salsa verde

3 tablespoons extra virgin olive oil
2 tablespoons red wine vinegar
1 teaspoon French whole-grain mustard
1 large handful flat-leaf (Italian) parsley
   leaves, chopped
3 cornichons or gherkins, diced

Rinse the chicken well, inside and out, and place in a large saucepan. Cover with water and add the onion, bouquet garni and a bit of sea salt. Bring to a boil, then reduce the heat to low and simmer for 1 hour. Add the vegetables and cook for another 30 minutes or until tender.

Meanwhile, make the salsa verde. Mix all the ingredients in a small bowl.

Remove the chicken and vegetables from the saucepan and place on a platter. Chop the chichen into pieces and discard the skin and bones. Serve with the salsa verde. Cooked Puy lentils are also nice served alongside.

PREP AHEAD

The vegetables can be peeled and prepared on the morning of serving and kept in a bowl of cold water to keep them from discoloring.

THE SKINNY

Poaching meat or poultry keeps the flesh juicy and tender but no oil or fat is needed. The piquant salsa verde is also healthy and complements the chicken's mild taste.

Pork tenderloin with charred tomato and chipotle chile sauce

preparation time 30 minutes / cooking time 30 minutes / serves 6

Authentic Mexican sauces use an ingenious technique called blackening. The onions and tomatoes are placed under the broiler or in a skillet and cooked until blackened. When pureed with chiles, cider vinegar, sugar and spices, it creates an amazing smoky tomato sauce.

2 pork tenderloins (18 ounces each)
1 tablespoon granulated sugar
1 teaspoon mild ground chile peppers, or to taste (ancho is nice but use any mild one)
fresh cilantro leaves and lime-pickled onion (see page 76), to serve
sea salt
black pepper

Red sauce

3 plum tomatoes, halved
1 small brown onion, thickly sliced
4 large clove garlics, unpeeled
1½ tablespoons apple cider vinegar
1 cup water
½ teaspoon dried wild oregano
⅛ teaspoon ground cumin
1 chipotle, skin and seeds removed
1½ tablespoons light brown sugar

To make the red sauce, preheat the broiler to high. Line a large baking sheet with foil. Arrange the tomato halves and onion slices on the baking sheet. Season with sea salt and freshly ground black pepper and broil for 10 minutes or until blackened. Remove and transfer to a blender or food processor.

Cook the garlic in their skins in a dry skillet over medium heat for 8 minutes or until blackened on all sides. Allow to cool a little, then peel and add to the tomato mixture. Add the vinegar, water, spices, chipotle, sugar and some sea salt. Puree until very smooth. Pour into a saucepan and cook over medium-low heat for 10 minutes to bring the flavors together.

Preheat a grill or grll pan to high. Rub the pork with the granulated sugar and ground chile peppers and season. grill for 3 minutes each side. Thickly slice the meat and serve with the red sauce. Top with the cilantro and pickled onion.

PREP AHEAD

The sauce can be made 4 days ahead and refrigerated. It also freezes well.

THE SKINNY

The tasty sauce is made primarily from charred tomatoes and vegetables and is quite healthy. Pork tenderloin is a very lean meat.

Slow-roasted pork with spice crust and pomegranate glaze

preparation time 15 minutes / cooking time 3 hours / serves 6

Aromatic spices and pomegranate molasses make an exotic sauce for this slow-roasted pork. Neck is a particularly lean cut that has enough marbling to slowly melt away during the slow-cooking process resulting in flaky tender shreds of meat. You could make basmati rice boiled with Puy (French) lentils or tri-color couscous to serve alongside.

1 teaspoon olive oil
3 ¼ pounds pork leg, shoulder or neck, trimmed of all external fat
1 large onion, roughly chopped
1 teaspoon cumin seeds, roughly crushed
1 teaspoon coriander seeds, roughly crushed
1 teaspoon fennel seeds, roughly crushed
1 teaspoon chile flakes
3 cloves garlic, smashed into a paste
1¾ cups water
4½ tablespoons pomegranate molasses
fresh pomegranate seeds and chopped flat-leaf (Italian) parsley, to serve
sea salt
black pepper

Preheat the oven to 300°F.

Heat the olive oil in a nonstick skillet over high heat. Season the pork well with sea salt and freshly ground black pepper, then sear on all sides until browned.

Place the onion in a large roasting pan. Mix all of the dry spices and garlic paste together with some sea salt and freshly ground black pepper in a small bowl. Rub this mixture all over the meat, then place the pork on top of the onion. Pour the water into the pan and cover tightly with foil. Roast for 2½ hours, then remove the foil. If the water has evaporated, add a bit more to the pan. Pour the pomegranate molasses over the pork and continue to roast, uncovered, for another 30 minutes or until the meat is tender and a sticky glaze has formed on top. Serve on a platter with the fresh pomegranate seeds and parsley scattered on top.

PREP AHEAD

Marinate the meat in the spice mixture the day before and refrigerate.

THE SKINNY

Always trim off any obvious fat on the outside of the meat. The marbling on the inside will melt away during the slow cooking.

Mustard rack of lamb with dried cherry and shallot port sauce

preparation time 15 minutes / marinating time 1 hour / cooking time 25–35 minutes / serves 4

Although you would consider rack of lamb off limits for skinny cooking, once the layer of fat is taken off, it's not such a calorie crusher. The lean tender fillet beneath gets sealed in with fresh thyme and mustard while it roasts. The port gravy is a fitting sauce for this elegant cut of meat.

4 racks (3 ribs each) of lamb, trimmed
  of most fat, and bones cleaned
2 cloves garlic, chopped
1 heaping tablespoon chopped thyme
2 tablespoons tawny or regular port
2 teaspoons olive oil
3 tablespoons Dijon mustard
smashed baby potatoes
  or celeriac puree, to serve
sea salt
black pepper

Dried cherry and shallot port sauce

1 cup tawny or regular port
2 tablespoons dried sour cherries,
  roughly chopped
2 teaspoons olive oil
2 shallots, finely chopped
1 tablespoon all-purpose flour
1 cup beef broth
1 tablespoon red currant jelly

Season the racks of lamb with sea salt and freshly ground black pepper and place in a bowl with the garlic and half the thyme. Pour the port over and allow to marinate for 1 hour or more (up to overnight) if you have time.

Preheat the oven to 400°F. Drain the meat dry and season all over. Heat the olive oil in a skillet over high heat until very hot and sear the lamb, fat side down, until golden. Place the lamb, fat side up, in a heavy-bottomed roasting pan. Rub the mustard all over the lamb and sprinkle with more seasoning and the remaining thyme. Roast for 15 minutes for rare, 20 minutes for medium and 25 minutes for well-done. Transfer the lamb to a wire rack placed over a baking sheet and cover loosely with foil to rest for 10 minutes. Reserve the roasting pan. The resting is important for perfect pink meat so do be sure to build in time to do this.

Meanwhile, make the dried cherry and shallot port sauce. Heat the port until boiling and add the cherries. Remove from the heat and allow to sit for 5 minutes.

Scrape out all the oil from the lamb roasting pan. Heat the olive oil in the roasting pan over medium heat, add the shallots and saute for a few minutes or until just soft. Add the flour and stir for 1 minute over medium heat, then add the port mixture and broth. Simmer for 5 minutes or until the sauce thickens. Add the red currant jelly and season. Remove from the heat. Serve the lamb with the sauce and the smashed potatoes or celeriac puree.

PREP AHEAD

The lamb can be seared and the sauce can be made using the oil that the lamb was seared in. Roast the lamb just before you want to eat.

THE SKINNY

Although a tiny bit of the lamb dripping is used to make the sauce, the dripping allows all the bits of flavor from the lamb to come through.

Mastering refrigerator pizza dough

Pizza doesn't have to be fattening. It all comes down to the cheese and meat toppings you choose. Just a little cheese tastes good but you don't need heaps of it. Same goes for the meat; a small taste is great but you don't need a lot. The dough, vegetables, meats and tomato sauce are all fairly skinny. Even though pizza dough is available at supermarkets, it's so much nicer to make your own. No one has time to make dough after work and then let it rise, so this method is perfect for a busy lifestyle. Using refrigerator dough, you can make it, refrigerate it for up to 3 days and just take out the portion you want 3 hours before using. It makes an inexpensive, healthy and fun dinner. The possibilities for variations are endless.There are millions of different pizza dough recipes but they don't vary much: yeast, water, flour, salt and olive oil. I prefer the Napoli-style pizza — bubbly soft with a crisp crust, not too thin and not too thick.

FLOUR Different varieties can produce entirely different results. Bread or all-purpose flours make a heavier dough and "00" (finely milled Italian flour) results in something softer.

OLIVE OIL If you like ultra-thin crisp pizza, then mixing olive oil into the dough will impart that brittle texture. Otherwise, use it to keep the dough moist while it rises.

YEAST Be sure to use active dry yeast not rapid rise (which leaves little time to develop flavor). Only a small amount (¼ teaspoon per 18 ounces) is required for slow-rising dough and it will give the pizza base more flavor and depth and create more air bubbles.

GETTING THE DOUGH RIGHT A light bubbly crisp dough comes down to this: soft light sticky dough equals an airy bubbly base; a heavy dry dough equals a solid heavy one. You want to aim for a slightly sticky light dough. But try not to get hung up on measuring, just add enough flour to the dough after the initial suggested amount so that you can mix or knead it together. After mixing it into a ball, oil your hands to work with it. Even if it's sticky (and it will be), persevere so you don't have to add too much flour. Using an electric mixer with a dough hook is a good option if you don't want to knead the dough by hand. It also allows you to work with a much stickier dough.

USE THE REFRIGERATOR TO RISE THE DOUGH The longer dough takes to rise, the more flavor it develops. Make sure the dough is oiled and covered in plastic wrap so it doesn't dry out and impede rising. When you want to use it over 3 days, take out the portion you need, let it come to room temperature, then make the pizzas.

PIZZA STONES Any oven can be used, but using a pizza stone results in crisper pizza than using a baking sheet. Put your pizza stone in a cold oven, then turn the temperature as high as it will go (stones need to go in a cold oven or they may crack).

PIZZA PEELS Although you can use a baking sheet to take the pizza in and out of the oven, a pizza peel is best. Cover it with polenta, flour or semolina and place your dough over it. They will be the "wheels" that allow the pizza to slide onto the stone.

Refrigerator pizza dough

preparation time 15 minutes / rising time 2–5 hours / makes six 10-inch-diameter bases

18 ounces (a little over 4 cups) oo flour,
   plus 3 tablespoons extra
1 teaspoon sea salt
1¾ cups warm water
¼ teaspoon dried active yeast
   (not rapid rise)
olive oil, for greasing

Place the flour and salt in the bowl of an electric mixer. Fill a measuring cup with the warm water. It should be "hand hot"; not so hot that you can't put your finger in but also not too lukewarm. Add the yeast, mix and wait about 5 minutes or so for little chunks to float up to the top. This is important because it means the yeast is working. Sometimes instant yeast can go off and it's infuriating to discover later. Always be sure and test it.

Fit the dough hook attachment to your mixer. Turn the motor on and slowly pour in the liquid. Knead until a dough forms. It should pull away completely at the base and come together as a ball. If it doesn't, slowly add up to 3 tablespoons of extra flour, a little at a time until it does. Continue kneading in the mixer for 5–7 minutes or until smooth and elastic.

Oil your hands, a bowl and a sheet of plastic wrap. Take out the dough, place in the bowl, oil the dough all over and cover with the oiled plastic. Place in the refrigerator for up to 3 days. (If you want to use the dough on the same day of making, skip the chilling and leave the dough to rise at room temperature until doubled in size.)

When you want to use it, take out the portion you want and let it double in size at room temperature. It should still be covered with plastic wrap and the surface of the dough should be oiled. The temperature of your kitchen will determine how quickly it rises. During the summer it may only take a couple of hours, but in winter it may take 4–5 hours. If you have a cold draughty kitchen, then turn on the oven for 1 minute, turn off the heat, then place the bowl inside for the dough rise.

Pizza with Italian sausage, peperoncini and sweet onions

preparation time 15 minutes / cooking time 35 minutes / chilling time 30 minutes /serves 4–6

This is my all-time favorite pizza. I usually buy low-fat Italian-style sausages made with chicken or turkey and I don't use a huge quantity either. If buying the pork variety, then make sure the percentage of lean is high. This makes 6 pizzas but if you only want to make 4, then you can refrigerate the extra dough for up to 3 days or, even better, use it to make garlic flat bread or Middle Eastern lavash with spices. Freeze the extra sauce.

Sauce

1 tablespoon olive oil
3 cloves garlic, thinly sliced
2 cans (14 ounces each) whole plum
   tomatoes
1 tablespoon tomato paste
2 teaspoons dried oregano
1 teaspoon sea salt

Pizza bases

1 recipe refrigerator pizza dough
   (see page 156), at room temperature
   and doubled in size
semolina flour or polenta, for dusting

Toppings

olive oil spray
3 lean sausages (turkey or pork),
   casings removed and meat crumbled
1 teaspoon fennel seeds
1 large pinch of chile flakes
½ cup shredded part-skim mozzarella
thinly sliced peperoncini (Italian pickled
   peppers) or roasted marinated
   pepper
2 white or red onions, thinly sliced
1 tablespoon fresh oregano leaves

To make the sauce, heat the olive oil in a saucepan over high heat. Add the garlic and saute until golden, about 3 minutes. Add the tomatoes and break up a bit with a spoon. Add the tomato paste. Sprinkle in the dried oregano and salt. Simmer until all the liquid has evaporated and the sauce has thickened nicely, 20–25 minutes. Scrape into a bowl, cool, then refrigerate until chilled. (It works best to make pizzas with cold sauce.)

If you have a pizza stone, place it on the lowest rack of your oven. Turn your oven up to the highest temperature it will go.

To prepare the sausage, heat a nonstick skillet sprayed with a tiny bit of olive oil over high heat. Add the sausage meat, fennel seeds and chile flakes and cook until it has browned a bit, breaking up the meat with a spoon. Remove from the heat.

To make the pizza bases, punch down the dough and divide into 6 pieces. Working with 1 piece at a time, roll out each piece on a lightly floured surface with a rolling pin to make a 10-inch-diameter round, about ¼-inch thick. Spread a teaspoon or so of the semolina on the pizza peel (or you can use a baking sheet without a rim). Place the pizza base on top and make sure it can move around. Spread a thin layer of the sauce over the pizza base, scatter over a little cheese, some sausage, a small handful of peperoncini and onion and finish with a sprinkle of oregano leaves. Slide the pizza onto the preheated pizza stone (if you don't have one, use a baking sheet), and cook for 4–5 minutes or until the base is crisp. Enjoy your pizza straight out of the oven, then make the next — that's part of the fun of homemade pizzas.

If you want to cook your pizzas all at once, then pan pizzas are the solution. You will need two large baking sheets with a rim — the ones I use are 14¼ x 10½-inch with a ¾-inch lip. Sprinkle the sheets with semolina. Take 4 portions of dough (you will need to save the remaining 2 portions of dough) and use 2 portions for each sheet. Roll out to ½ inch thick and place on the sheets. Add the sauce and toppings and bake in a preheated 425°F oven for 12–15 minutes or until the crust is golden. (Serves 4.)

OTHER GREAT COMBINATIONS

Spinach, ham and feta

Grilled eggplant, garlic and pecorino

Thinly sliced white onion, tomatoes, fresh oregano and part-skim mozzarella

Mushroom, asiago cheese, garlic and chile flakes

Tomatoes, goat cheese and pancetta

Fresh figs, pancetta and a small amount of Gorgonzola or low-fat mozzarella

Thin base of pesto, chicken, red onion and part-skim mozzarella

Smoky Spanish beef stew with cannellini beans

preparation time 15 minutes / **cooking time** 1¼ hours / **serves** 6

Seared chunks of beef are simmered in a spicy tomato, pepper and red wine sauce until fork-tender. It's best to buy a whole piece of beef and cut it yourself rather than buy packs of stewing steak. The pieces are often too small and cook up rubbery. This looks like a long list of ingredients, but it doesn't take more than 15 minutes to put together. Try using Spanish roasted piquillo peppers, otherwise regular jarred ones are fine.

2 roasted red peppers

2 tablespoons olive oil

1¾ pound beef (stewing cut), cut into
   2-inch chunks

1 large yellow onion, chopped

2 cloves garlic, chopped

2 tablespoons smoked paprika

1 cup red wine

2 tablespoons sherry vinegar

2 tablespoons honey

15 small carrots, scrubbed and trimmed

¾ cup tomato puree

2 cans (15 ounces each)cannellini
   beans, drained

chopped flat-leaf (Italian) parsley,
   to serve

sea salt

black pepper

If you're not using jarred roasted peppers and you want to roast your own, place two bell peppers on a baking sheet and broil, turning occasionally, until blackened and blistered all over. Alternatively, place the peppers directly on top of a low gas flame and turn frequently until blackened. Transfer to a bowl, cover with plastic wrap and allow to cool. Peel and remove the seeds but do not wash the flesh.

Place the roasted peppers in a food processor with any juices and puree until smooth.

Heat 1 tablespoon of the olive oil in a large heavy-bottomed saucepan over high heat. Season the beef with sea salt and freshly ground black pepper and brown in batches.

Remove from the pan and set aside.

Reduce the heat to medium, add the onion, garlic and remaining olive oil to the same pan, season and saute for 6–8 minutes or until softened. Add the paprika, roasted pepper puree, wine, vinegar, honey, carrots and tomato puree. Cover with a lid and cook over low heat for 1 hour or until the beef is fork-tender. Just as the beef is ready, add the beans and warm through. Taste for seasoning. Serve with a sprinkling of parsley.

PREP AHEAD

The stew can be made 2–3 days ahead and refrigerated or frozen.

THE SKINNY

Stews such as this are low in fat as most of the sauce is just tasty tomatoes and wine. The beans and carrots make it a one-pot dish.

Chicken, apricot and tomato tagine

preparation time 15 minutes / cooking time 50 minutes / serves 6

When my family and I visited Morocco a couple of years ago, I was surprised at how rustic the tagines were. Night after night, eating out at restaurants, the same trio of carrot, lamb on the bone and onions appeared. It was nothing like the exotic spice-aromatic stews I had read about and cooked. A friend told me later that you need to be invited to someone's house in order to get the dishes one reads about. Not having that luxury at my disposal I decided to carry on with my own interpretations and this is one of my favorites. Serve some couscous mixed with herbs alongside.

2 teaspoons olive oil

12 small boneless, skinless chicken thighs, trimmed of all fat, halved

2 yellow onions, thinly sliced

2-inch piece of fresh ginger, finely grated

3 cloves garlic, finely chopped

1 teaspoon saffron threads

1 teaspoon boiling water

1 teaspoon ground ginger

1 teaspoon ground cumin

1 large cinnamon stick

2 tablespoons tomato paste

2 cups chicken broth

12 plump dried apricots, cut into quarters

2 tablespoons honey

juice of 1¼ lemons, plus lemon wedges to serve

finely chopped cilantro and steamed couscous, to serve

sea salt

black pepper

Heat 1 teaspoon of the olive oil over high heat in a large saucepan. Season the chicken well with sea salt and freshly ground black pepper and sear until browned on both sides. Remove from the saucepan and set aside.

Add the remaining oil to the saucepan, along with the onion, ginger, garlic and some salt and pepper to taste. Saute for 10 minutes or until the onion has softened. Slightly crush the saffron, pour the boiling water over it and allow to infuse for a minute. Add the saffron mixture and all of the spices to the saucepan and cook for 1 minute or until aromatic. Add the tomato paste, broth, apricots, honey, lemon juice
and chicken. Cook over medium-low heat for 30 minutes or until the chicken is tender. Sprinkle with the cilantro and serve with the lemon wedges and couscous.

PREP AHEAD

The tagine can be made 2 days ahead and refrigerated or frozen. Gently reheat in a saucepan and add a little broth or water if it's too thick.

THE SKINNY

Tagine sauces are composed mainly of spice, onion and broth, making them very healthy choices as well as gorgeous meals.

Hainanese chicken with sweet soy and chile dipping sauce

preparation time 15 minutes / cooking time 10 minutes / standing time 1 hour / serves 4

This Malaysian dish originated in China but is now eaten by both cultures. A whole chicken is poached and then eaten with garlic rice, cucumber and a sweet soy and ginger-spiked sauce. The meat poaches beautifully white and retains its juices. It's important you use the right size chicken for this. If it's bigger than 2 pounds 6 ounces, then up the initial boiling time to 15 minutes instead of 10 minutes.

9 cups water
1 whole chicken (preferably free-range)
2 teaspoons vegetable oil
2 cloves garlic, finely chopped
1 cup basmati or long-grain rice
2 small cucumbers, shaved into ribbons
   with a vegetable peeler
1 small handful cilantro leaves, roughly
   chopped

Sweet soy and chile dipping sauce

1 thumb-sized red chile, seeds removed
   and chopped
½ clove garlic, chopped
½-inch piece of fresh ginger, finely
   chopped
1½ tablespoons Indonesian sweet soy
   sauce (kecap manis), or 3 tablespoons
   regular soy sauce mixed with
   1 tablespoon light brown sugar
2 teaspoons rice vinegar
2 teaspoons superfine sugar

Bring the water to a boil in a large stockpot or deep saucepan. Add the chicken (it should be covered completely with water) and simmer gently for 10 minutes. Turn off the heat but leave the pot on the stove and cover with a lid. Leave to sit for 1 hour.

Meanwhile, make the sweet soy and chile dipping sauce. (If you don't want to chop all the ingredients by hand, you could pulse them in the food processor.) Combine all of the ingredients in a small bowl. Set aside.

About 10 minutes before the chicken is done, heat the vegetable oil in a saucepan over medium heat, add the garlic and saute until golden. Add the rice and stir for 1 minute. Ladle in enough of the chicken-poaching liquid to cover the rice by ½ inch. Cover with a lid, reduce the heat to low and cook for 8–10 minutes or until al dente.

Remove the chicken from the pot. Discard the skin and chop the meat into pieces, pull the meat from the bones (see Note). Arrange the chicken on a platter with the cucumber and cilantro. Serve with the rice and dipping sauce.

NOTE You can reserve the poaching liquid and bones and simmer for 1 hour with a chopped onion, carrot and celery stalk to make a delicious broth.

PREP AHEAD

The dipping sauce can be made on the morning of serving but everything else should be done 1–2 hours before eating.

THE SKINNY

Poaching chicken is a beautiful method for low-fat cooking and delicious juicy meat.

Skinny Sweets

Pineapple and mint granita

preparation time 30 minutes / freezing time 3 hours / makes 52 fluid ounces

Granita is brilliant because you don't need an ice-cream machine. The fruit puree and sugar syrup are poured into a shallow pan and scraped three times during the freezing process. The result is granular pieces of fruity ice. This makes a big granita but if you are going to the trouble to make it, you may as well make a big batch. Baby pineapples are sweeter than the bigger versions and the fresh mint is a refreshing counterpart.

1⅓ cups water
1 cup plus 2 tablespoons superfine sugar
2¼ pounds chopped pineapple
¼ cup lime juice
1 large handful mint leaves, finely chopped tropical fruit, such as mango or papaya, chopped, to serve

Bring the water and sugar to a boil in a saucepan and simmer for 5 minutes or until slightly syrupy. Allow to cool completely.

Puree the pineapple in a food processor, then push through a fine sieve to create a smooth puree. Discard any pulp in the sieve. Mix the cooled syrup, lime juice and mint with the puree. Pour into a shallow 13 x 9-inch metal or glass pan and place in the freezer.

After 2 hours, scrape the mixture with a fork. When breaking up the ice crystals, make long scrapes, raking the fork down the mixture repeatedly. Avoid mixing it up, which will result in a smooth texture more like sherbet. Freeze again for another 30 minutes, then repeat scraping and freezing two more times until grainy crystals have formed.

Serve with the tropical fruit.

PREP AHEAD

This will keep for 2 weeks in the freezer in an airtight container.

THE SKINNY

A clever way to get a good quota of fruit into you. Granted, it has a bit of sugar, but it's still pretty healthy.

Little cocoa kisses

preparation time 10 minutes / **cooking time** 1 hour / **makes** 60 tiny bites (depends on how big you make them)

These petite meringues are quite easy to make. If you can make them last, they're quite a handy sweet snack. You can spoon them onto the baking sheet, or do as I do and pipe them: fill a large zip-lock plastic bag with the mixture and snip off a corner with scissors. I like to pipe them small with a little curl at the top.

Meringues have a few simple rules for success and, if you follow them, you won't run into problems. First start with a very clean bowl — grease will chemically react with the egg whites and inhibit volume. Next, don't allow any yolk to get into the whites because any fat will, again, cause the whites to become foamy instead of glossy. Older eggs (2 weeks or so) work better than fresh ones and the most important consideration of all is that the whites need to be at room temperature.

2 large egg whites, at room temperature
4½ ounces superfine sugar
1 teaspoon unsweetened cocoa powder
½ teaspoon vanilla extract
pinch of salt

Preheat the oven to 235°F. Line two baking sheets with parchment paper.

Place the egg white in the bowl of an electric mixer and beat with a tiny pinch of salt for 1–2 minutes or until soft peaks form. Add the sugar a tablespoonful at a time until incorporated. Keep beating for 1–2 minutes or until stiff glossy peaks form. Sift the cocoa over, add the vanilla extract and gently fold into the mixture.

Spoon or pipe heaped teaspoons onto the baking sheets. Bake for 1 hour. Remove and allow to cool on the baking sheets. Store in an airtight container.

PREP AHEAD

The kisses can be made 3 days ahead and stored in an airtight container.

THE SKINNY

With only sugar and a tiny bit of cocoa, these are an ideal skinny treat with almost no fat. It's good to have something like this around when you get a sweet craving instead of eating something much worse.

Chewy meringues with blackberries and Greek-style yogurt

preparation time 20 minutes / **cooking time** 35 minutes / **cooling time** 2 hours / **makes** 16

Meringues can be prepared in many ways. If you cook them on low heat for hours, they become powdery; if cooked with a combination of high and low, you get a chewy toffee centre with a crisp exterior. These are the latter, which are nice on their own or as a full-on dessert.

⅔ cup eggwhite (from about 4 eggs), at
   room temperature
¾ cup plus two tablespoons superfine
   sugar
2 teaspoons cornstarch
1 teaspoon white distilled vinegar
¾ pound blackberries or other berries
1⅛ tablespoons confectioners' sugar
1 cup low-fat Greek-style yogurt
tiny mint leaves, for garnishing

Preheat the oven to 300°F.
Line two large baking sheets with parchment paper.
   Place the egg white in the bowl of an electric mixer and beat until soft peaks form. Add the superfine sugar a tablespoon at a time until incorporated. Keep whisking for 1–2 minutes or until stiff glossy peaks form. Sift the cornstarch over, add the vinegar and gently fold into the mixture. Place 16 dollops of meringue, 3–4 inches in size, leaving plenty of space in between. Reduce the oven to 235°F and bake for 35 minutes. Turn the oven off and allow the meringues to cool for a couple of hours. This is an important step because if you take them out at this point, they will be soft; the cooling process makes them crisp. To serve, gently crush the berries in a bowl with the back of a fork and mix in the confectioners' sugar until dissolved. Serve the meringues with the berries and yogurt, garnished with the mint.

PREP AHEAD

These will keep for 4–5 days in an airtight container.

THE SKINNY

Although meringues have a lot of sugar, they don't have any egg yolks or butter. The low-fat Greek-style yogurt also replaces fat-laden whipped cream.

Caramelized broiled mango with mint

preparation time 10 minutes / cooking time 5 minutes / serves 4

This low-effort dessert works well with tropical fruit, such as mangoes or pineapple slices. It's the perfect ending to complement an Asian meal. Vanilla paste, which is a little pot of scraped seeds, is sold in some supermarkets. It allows you to use a little without much waste.

2 large ripe but firm mangoes
½ teaspoon vanilla paste (or ½ vanilla bean, split and seeds scraped)
3 tablespoons superfine sugar
low fat frozen yogurt or low-fat raspberry sorbet and mint leaves, to serve

Slice the cheeks off the mangoes. Lightly score a criss-cross pattern on the cut sides. Add the vanilla paste or seeds to the sugar. Mix well and spread across the mangoes. Place under a hot broiler and cook for 3–4 minutes or until the sugar caramelizes. Remove and serve in bowls with a scoop of frozen yogurt or sherbet with the mint leaves scattered over.

PREP AHEAD

The vanilla sugar can be made a couple of days ahead and stored in an airtight container. The mangoes are best broiled just before serving.

THE SKINNY

Fresh vanilla seeds give fruit a luxurious tropical boost. Frozen yogurt or sorbet is a low-calorie partner for fruit, and you won't feel like you've missed out on a sweet ending.

Rhubarb and strawberry compote

preparation time 5 minutes / cooking time 15 minutes / serves 4

This makes a great dessert with Greek-style yogurt, or use it as a topping for chewy meringues (see page 170). The strawberries' sweetness foils the rhubarb's sharp edge.

14 ounces thin rhubarb, leaves trimmed,
   stalks cut into 2 inch lengths
6 ounces strawberries, shucked
   and halved
2 tablespoons superfine sugar
2 tablespoons orange juice
1 vanilla bean, split and seeds scraped
low-fat Greek-style yogurt, to serve

Preheat the oven to 375°F.
   Place the rhubarb and strawberries in a large shallow baking dish. Sprinkle the sugar over and drizzle over the orange juice. Add the vanilla seeds and mix well to distribute. Roast for 15 minutes or until just tender.
   Serve warm with the yogurt.

PREP AHEAD

The rhubarb should be roasted shortly before serving. You can chop it 2 hours before but don't mix it until just before roasting.

THE SKINNY

Warm compotes are comforting sweets in the winter and amazingly healthy.

Little elderflower sparkling berry gelatins

preparation time 15 minutes / setting time 5 hours / serves 6

It's not difficult to make your own gelatin desert using gelatin sheets or powder and flavored juice, wine or cordial. It's particularly refreshing in the summer and a wonderful vehicle for fresh berries and other fruit. Elderflower cordial, the quintessential English drink, is made from crushed elderflowers, lemon and sugar. Its perfumed scent is concentrated and meant to be mixed with water, one part to ten, so only a small amount is needed here.

6 gold-strength gelatine sheets or powder
10 tablespoons elderflower cordial
⅔ cup superfine sugar
2 cups Champagne or sparkling white wine
½ pound mixed berries, such as halved strawberries, blueberries or blackberries
low-fat Greek-style yogurt, to serve

Soak the gelatine leaves in cold water until soft, about 5 minutes.

Heat the elderflower cordial with the sugar in a saucepan over low heat for 5 minutes or until the sugar has dissolved.

Drain the gelatin, discarding the water and squeeze out the excess water with your hands.

Add to the warm cordial mixture and stir over low heat until the gelatin has dissolved (if using gelatin powder add directly to the cordial mixture here). Don't allow to boil but just keep at a low simmer. Remove from the heat and allow to cool a bit.

Pour in the Champagne and mix. Divide the berries among six 8-ounce custard cups, small teacups or any small container that is at least 7 ounces. Pour half of the liquid mixture in and refrigerate for 1 hour.

Remove from the refrigerator and pour the remaining liquids into the ramekins. This two-step process will keep the berries in the middle of the mixture instead of them floating to the top. Refrigerate again for another 4 hours or until firmly set.

Serve with the low-fat Greek-style yogurt or just on its own.

PREP AHEAD

The gelatins can be prepared 2 days ahead and stored in the refrigerator.

THE SKINNY

The berries keep the gelatin bright and healthy.

Baked apples stuffed with dates, cinnamon and oats

preparation time 10 minutes / cooking time 40 minutes / serves 4

For a light dessert, these baked apples are quite decadent. Cinnamon-spiced oats mixed with dates, lemon zest and dark brown sugar create a crisp topping without large amounts of butter. The sweet wine keeps the apple flesh soft and turns into a lovely sauce. Top with vanilla frozen yogurt or a small spoonful of dulce de leche sauce.

4 apples
finely grated zest of 1 lemon and juice of
   ½ lemon
1½ teaspoons unsalted butter,
   at room temperature
5 tablespoons plus 1 teaspoon dark
   brown sugar
2 large fresh dates, pitted and finely
   chopped
1 tablespoon all-purpose flour
2 teaspoons ground cinnamon
2 tablespoons rolled oats
⅔ cup Sauternes, muscat or other
   dessert wine
2 tablespoons sliced almonds
frozen vanilla yogurt or
   dulce de leche sauce, to serve
   (optional)

Preheat the oven to 375°F. Halve the apples crosswise and remove the core with a melon baller. Rub the cut sides with the lemon juice. In a small bowl, mix together the butter, sugar, dates, flour, cinnamon, oats and lemon zest. Divide among the apple halves, stuffing the mixture inside the cavity of each. Nestle the apple halves into a baking dish that fits them snugly. Pour in the wine, sprinkle with the almonds, cover with foil and bake for 20 minutes. Remove the foil and bake for another 20 minutes or until the apples are tender, golden and crisp.

Serve on their own, with the frozen yogurt or a drizzle of duche de leche sauce.

PREP AHEAD

The apples can be filled 4 hours ahead but rub well with lemon juice to prevent them from browning.

THE SKINNY

The dates keep the amount of sugar and butter down, while adding sweetness and texture. A tiny drizzle of dulce de leche is okay — it's made from sugar and milk but, unlike caramel sauce, there is no butter.

Frozen passionfruit yogurt ice cream

preparation time 10 minutes / cooling time 1 hour / freezing time 5 hours / makes 4 cups

Once you make this, you will never buy frozen yogurt again. It's so easy, delicious and best of all, fat-free! You will need to use thick Greek-style yogurt to make this. I experimented with both the 2% as well as the 0% and you will be glad to know there wasn't any difference in texture or taste. If you don't have access to the thick Greek variety, then place plain low-fat yogurt in a fine sieve and leave for 1 day in the refrigerator. The remaining thick mixture is the same as thick Greek-style yogurt, but you will most likely need 4 cups if making your own. Any flavor fruit can be substituted in place of the passionfruit.

12 passionfruit
⅔ cup superfine sugar
3¼ (26 ounces) 0% Greek-style yogurt
1 vanilla bean, split and seeds scraped

Halve the passionfruit and scoop out the pulp. Strain the pulp through a fine sieve, reserving the juice and 2 tablespoons of the seeds. You will need 10 tablespoons of juice. Heat the juice with the sugar and simmer for 5 minutes or until slightly syrupy. Mix the yogurt, vanilla seeds and passionfruit syrup in a bowl. Place in the refrigerator for 2 hours, then churn in an ice cream machine according to the manufacturer's instructions until thick, then add the reserved seeds. Freeze in a covered container until firm.

NOTE To make strawberry or raspberry frozen yogurt, puree 14 ounces of your chosen fruit in a food processor, then push through a fine sieve. Discard the solids and mix the puree with the sugar and vanilla. Stir to dissolve, then mix into the yogurt. Chopped bits of extra fruit can be mixed in when it has finished churning.

PREP AHEAD

The frozen yogurt will keep for up to 1 month in the freezer.

THE SKINNY

Made with fat-free yogurt, this is the skinniest iced treat you can make, so enjoy! Unlike ice cream, there are no eggs or cream.

Raspberry sorbet

preparation time 10 minutes / cooking time 7 minutes / chilling time 1 hour 20 minutes / freezing time 3 hours / makes 4 cups

There is no better way to put punnets of summer fruit to good use than making sorbet. I've included a little light corn syrup. Without it, homemade sorbet can be a bit grainy, so put in a few tablespoons to keep it velvety smooth. If you don't have an ice cream machine, then you can make a granita instead (see pineapple and mint granita on page 168 for technique).

¾ cup plus 2 tablespoons water
9 ounces superfine sugar
3 tablespoons light corn syrup
1¼ pound fresh or frozen raspberries
1 tablespoon lemon juice
fresh fruit, to serve

Bring the water, sugar and light corn syrup to a boil in a small saucepan over medium-high heat, then cook for 5–7 minutes or until it is a thin syrup. Pour into a bowl and allow to cool, then refrigerate for 20 minutes or until chilled.

Meanwhile, mash the raspberries with the lemon juice, then push through a fine sieve and discard the seeds.

Stir the puree into the cold syrup. Return to the fridge and chill for another 1 hour. Churn in an ice cream machine according to the manufacturer's instructions until thick, then freeze in an airtight container.

Serve with fresh berries, chopped pineapple or mango.

PREP AHEAD

The sorbet can be frozen for up to 1 month.

THE SKINNY

Sorbet makes a perfect sweet treat, instead of ice cream, and this one is packed with fruit.

Roasted plums with star anise and cinnamon

preparation time 10 minutes / cooking time 20 minutes / serves 4

Aromatic spices, vanilla and orange juice flavor these baked plums for an exotic warm fruit dessert. Serve with frozen mango sorbet or Greek-style yogurt for a treat after Middle Eastern or Asian food.

6 small tomedium red plums, halved

3 star anise

2 cinnamon sticks

juice of 2 large oranges

2 tablespoons honey

2 tablespoons light brown sugar

1 teaspoon vanilla paste or ½ vanilla bean, split and seeds scraped

low-fat mango sorbet or Greek-style yogurt, to serve

Preheat the oven to 350°F. Place the plums, cut side up, in a baking dish in one layer. Mix the remaining ingredients except the sorbet in a small bowl to combine. Pour over the fruit and bake for 20 minutes or until golden and bubbling. Serve with the sorbet or yogurt.

PREP AHEAD

The plums can be baked for three-quarters of the cooking time, then finished off just before serving.

THE SKINNY

With the exception of sugar, there isn't anything else too high in calories in this dessert.

Peach Melba

preparation time 10 minutes / cooking time 10 minutes / serves 4

The scarlet raspberry sauce and bright orange peaches are a feast for your eyes as well as your stomach. Stone fruit takes on a silky character when poached and there is no better way to prepare summer's bounty. It's important to use good tasting ripe fruit for this. If your peaches are hard, let them ripen at room temperature for a few days before using.

2 cups water

⅓ cup superfine sugar

4 freestone (slipstone) peaches,
   ripe but not too soft

½ pound fresh or frozen raspberries

low-fat frozen yogurt, to serve

mint leaves, to garnish

Combine the water and ⅓ cup of the sugar in a saucepan over low heat and stir until the sugar dissolves.

Make two light incisions, forming a cross at the base of each peach. Increase the heat to medium, add the peaches and poach for 10 minutes. Remove from the liquid and peel with your hands. Halve and remove the pits. If you find this tricky, as sometimes the pits stick a little, hold the fruit with a paper towel, pull and firmly twist each pit until it comes loose.

Mash the raspberries with the remaining sugar, then push through a fine sieve and discard the seeds.

Arrange the peaches in dessert bowls and spoon the raspberry sauce over each. Top with a scoop of frozen yogurt and mint leaves.

PREP AHEAD

The peaches can be poached and peeled the day before but store in the poaching syrup in the refrigerator until needed. The raspberry sauce can also be made 1 day ahead.

THE SKINNY

Normally this would be served with ice cream, but frozen yogurt won't leave you lacking anything. The fruit and sauce are fat-free and very low in sugar as well.

Apple and pear chips with cinnamon and lemon sugar

preparation time 10 minutes / cooking time 45 minutes / makes about 60 rings

It sounds quite earnest to say you're going to make your own dried fruit, but once you see how easy and cheap it is, you'll be hooked. Try other fruits such as pineapple, sliced strawberries or raspberries. You will need a mandoline (inexpensive plastic ones are easy to get hold of and work very well).

2 Granny Smith apples
2 firm pears (Comice, Bartlett or any bigger variety)
juice of 1 lemon
2 tablespoons confectioners' sugar

Preheat the oven to 200°F. Line two baking sheets with silicone baking mats or parchment paper. Use a mandoline to slice the fruit into ⅛-inch-thick slices, going all the way through the core and place in a large bowl. Add the lemon juice, then sprinkle with the sugar. Gently toss to combine, being careful they don't break. Place on the baking sheets in a single layer. Bake for 45 minutes or until they are chewy and fairly dry (the pears may take up to 20 minutes longer depending on what variety you use). Remove from the oven and peel them from the baking sheet so they don't stick. Cool on a wire rack, then store immediately in an airtight container.

PREP AHEAD

These will keep for 3 days in an airtight container.

THE SKINNY

Low in fat and a perfect sweet snack. Pack them in your handbag or work lunchbox so you're not tempted with other more "dangerous" nibbles lurking in the vending machines.

Skinny tangerine dreamsicle lollies

preparation time 10 minutes / cooking time 15 minutes / freezing time 2 hours / serves 6

As a child, my favorite popsicle (or lollie as we call it in Britain) was tangerine dreamsicle. It's vanilla ice cream coated in an intense tangerine sherbet. This skinny interpretation is very close in taste to it and doesn't take more than 10 minutes to make.

2⅔ cups freshly squeezed tangerine or orange juice
7 tablespoons superfine sugar
¾ cup low-fat Greek-style yogurt

Combine the juice and ⅓ cup of the sugar in a saucepan and stir over medium heat until the sugar dissolves. Simmer for 15 minutes or until reduced by half. Cool to room temperature.

Combine the yogurt and remaining sugar.

Divide half of the juice mixture among six 3½-ounce popsicle molds. Top with the yogurt, then pour in the remaining juice mixture. Freeze for 2 hours or until firm.

PREP AHEAD

The popsicles can be frozen for up to 1 month.

THE SKINNY

Enjoy an icy skinny treat that tastes like ice cream with low sugar and hardly any fat.

Chianti and anise poached pears

preparation time 10 minutes / cooking time 30 minutes / serves 4

Anise seed has a licorice taste very similar to fennel but sweeter. When added to red wine with vanilla seeds it makes an exquisite poaching elixir for pears. My favorite type of pears are Comice, with sweet flesh and big chubby bottoms, but other varieties can be used. Be sure to use a small saucepan that keeps the pears snug while poaching.

3 cups Chianti or other Italian red wine
¾ cup plus 2 tablespoons superfine sugar
1 large strip orange zest
1 large strip lemon zest
1 teaspoon anise seeds or fennel seeds
1 vanilla bean, split and seeds scraped
4 Comice or other large firm pears, peeled
Greek-style yogurt or low-fat crème fraîche, to serve

Bring the wine, sugar, citrus zests, anise seeds and vanilla bean and seeds to a boil in a large saucepan. Reduce the heat to a low simmer and add the pears. Cook for 20–25 minutes or until the pears can easily be pierced with a skewer. The cooking time will vary slightly depending on the size of the pears. Use a slotted spoon to transfer the pears to a deep-sided dish, just large enough to hold the pears. Keep warm.

Strain the poaching liquid and pour it back into the saucepan. Cook over medium-high heat for 5 minutes or until reduced and slightly syrupy. Pour over the pears.

To serve, place a pear in a shallow bowl with 2 generous tablespoons of the syrup spooned over. A dollop of Greek-style yogurt or low-fat crème fraîche is also delicious eaten alongside.

PREP AHEAD

The pears can be poached and stored in their poaching liquid in the refrigerator overnight. Gently reheat the pears in their liquid, then remove the pears and reduce the sauce to a syrup.

THE SKINNY

The red wine and spiced poaching liquid gives the pears a depth and turns this dessert into a sticky skinny syrup to pour over the pears.

Lemon angel food cake

preparation time 15 minutes / cooking time 30 minutes / serves 8

The whipped egg white makes this angel food cake as light as a cloud and it is delicious with fresh berries or even a little drizzle of confectioners' sugar mixed with water. For a skinny trifle, layer leftover chunks of cake with berry coulis and Greek-style yogurt.

1½ cups egg white (from about 12 eggs), at room temperature
1¼ teaspoons cream of tartar
1 cup plus 2 tablespoons superfine sugar
2 tablespoons finely grated lemon zest
1 teaspoon vanilla extract
4½ ounces cake flour
berry or passionfruit coulis or low-fat Greek-style yogurt and fresh fruit, to serve

Preheat the oven to 350°F. Place the eggwhite in the bowl of an electric mixer and beat on medium speed until frothy, then add the cream of tartar. Increase the speed to high and, when the whites start getting fluffy, slowly spoon in the sugar until all of it is incorporated and stiff glossy peaks form. Fold in the zest and vanilla.

Remove the bowl from the mixer. Using a large metal spoon, sift one-third of the flour over the mixture and fold it in. Be gentle but quick so the whites don't deflate. Add the remaining flour in two more batches, then pour into an ungreased 10-inch round angel food cake pan, tube cake pan or non-fluted Bundt cake pan. Run a knife through the batter to make sure there aren't big air pockets.

Bake on the center oven rack for 30 minutes or until a skewer comes out clean. Remove from the oven and turn the pan upside down on the counter. This is important otherwise the cake will deflate. Allow to cool completely, about 2 hours.

Run a knife around the side and base to remove the cake from the pan. Serve with your choice of accompaniments.

PREP AHEAD

The cake will keep covered for a couple of days.

THE SKINNY

With the exception of the sugar, this is a pretty healthy sweet. If you're craving a slice of cake, this is completely guilt-free.

Acknowledgments

This book wouldn't have been possible without the help of so many people. It all started with Kay Scarlett, who commissioned this to follow *Meals in Heels*. You are a class act and left some big shoes to fill. The time I had to work with you will always be cherished.

Kylie Walker, I am very thankful to you picking up the reins on this project, being so supportive and making room for the photographs in the budget.

Emilia Toia, your masterful eye for design and sharp ideas are so impressive. Yet again, you've taken my recipes and created a jaw-dropping book.

Gabriella Sterio, your attention to detail and careful management of this have not gone unnoticed. Thank you for putting so much hard work in with such a positive attitude. Even though we were halfway across the world from each other, I always felt confident everything was swimming along. You are an amazing editor.

Belinda So, I knew I was in safe hands with you on the job, editing my text. The tiniest of details never miss your eyes and you really understand what I'm trying to do. It meant a lot to me to have you working on this after *Meals in Heels*.

Maja Smend, your photos are beautiful and I always enjoy food styling with you. You're not afraid to push the boundaries and get the perfect photograph.

Kathy Kordalis and Donna Laveran, thank you so much for all of your help testing recipes. Your chopping, washing up and suggestions were so appreciated. It was more fun than work.

Sarah Birks, thank you for pulling my props together with your eagle eye for design and good taste. It was you who cemented the idea for this book in my head. I always love working with you.

Megan Hess, your illustrations are gorgeous and oh so glamorous. Thanks, once again, for contributing such lovely work.

Christine Osmond and Murdoch test kitchen, I can sleep at night knowing you have been through the recipes in here with a fine-tooth comb. I feel very fortunate to have such a resource like you for my book.

Pat, Liam and Riley, I couldn't have done this book without your voracious appetites, love and support. Thank God you're always up for something new.

ATRIA PACKERBACK

A Division of Simon & Schuster, Inc.
1230 Avenue of the Americas
New York, NY 10020

First Atria Paperback edition July 2012

ATRIA PAPERBACK and colophon are trademarks of Simon & Schuster, Inc.

For information about special discounts for bulk purchases,
please contact Simon & Schuster Special Sales at
1-866-506-1949 or business@simonandschuster.com.

The Simon & Schuster Speakers Bureau can bring authors
to your live event. For more information or to book an event,
contact the Simon & Schuster Speakers Bureau at
1-866-248-3049 or visit our website at www.simonspeakers.com.

Manufactured in China

10 9 8 7 6 5 4 3 2 1

Library of Congress Cataloging-in-Publication Data
Joyce, Jennifer.
   Skinny meals in heels : prep-ahead, figure-friendly dishes for the busy home chef / by Jennifer Joyce.
      p. cm.
   Includes index.
   1. Quick and easy cooking.
   2. Low-fat diet--Recipes. I. Title.
   TX833.5.J69 2012
   641.5´55—dc23   2012021235

ISBN 978-1-4516-8507-7
ISBN 978-1-4516-8508-4 (ebook)

IMPORTANT: Those who might be at risk from the effects of salmonella poisoning (the elderly, pregnant
women, young children and those suffering from immune deficiency diseases) should consult their doctor
with any concerns about eating raw eggs.

OVEN GUIDE: You may find cooking times vary depending on the oven you are using. For fan-forced ovens,
as a general rule, set the oven temperature to 35°F lower than indicated in the recipe.